ATTACKING THE 3-3-5 DEFENSE WITH THE I OFFENSE

Leo Hand

ISBN: 1-58518-952-9
Library of Congress Control Number: 2005938034
Book layout and diagrams: Deborah Oldenburg
Cover design: Jeanne Hamilton
Front cover photo: Stephen Dunn/Getty Images

Coaches Choice
P.O. Box 1828
Monterey, CA 93942
www.coacheschoice.com

Dedication

For Travis and the beautiful woman who gave him life.

Acknowledgments

Thanks to Tony Shaw for giving me the opportunity to coach in Texas.

Thanks to Jim Murphy, Don Kloppenberg, and Will Shaw for all they taught me at Long Beach City College.

Thanks to Al Baldock for all that he taught me about offense.

Thanks to the wonderful people of the Zuni and Navajo Nations who taught me much more than I taught them during the seven years I lived with them.

Thanks to Joe Griffin for giving me one of the best coaching jobs in California.

Thanks to all of the splendid young men whom I have been privileged to coach.

Thanks to all of the great coaches whom I have been fortunate to have worked with and coached against.

Thanks to the offspring whose ancestors endured the Middle Passage and the Long Walk for all of the contributions that they have made to the greatest game of all.

Thanks to Howard Wells and Ron Detinger for giving me the chance to coach at El Paso High School.

Thanks to Allan Sepkowitz for giving me the opportunity to coach at Andress High School.

Thanks to Knifewing, whose music inspired the words of this book.

Thanks to Herman Masin, editor of Scholastic Coach, for all of his help and suggestions during the past 30 years.

Thanks to Dr. James A. Peterson for all of his help and encouragement.

Contents

Introduction

The modern 3-3-5 defenses is an evolutionary by-product of innovations that have occurred in an attempt to stop the spread offense. Versus the spread, the 3-3-5 has proven itself to be a great defense. During the last couple of years, however, a new offensive trend is beginning to emerge, which is a renaissance of two-back offenses. This tendency is particularly true in the NFL. This trend has resulted because many spread formation coaches have become discontented with the productivity of their running games. Trends that result in the chess game between the Xs and Os have always been cyclical, and it is not a new phenomena to resurrect strategies and tactics from the past in an attempt to upset the prosperity of the present. If the trend toward two-back offenses continues, the modern 3-3-5 will have to go through an evolution of its own and deal with the its many unresolved weaknesses versus two-back offenses.

Probably the most popular two-back offense to experience a rebirth is the I offense. The primary reason for this is the versatility of the offense. The I offense is:

- A two-back system that can be expanded to a three or four back system, or reduced to the appearance of an aceback system.
- A system that can involve one, two, three, or no wide receivers.
- A system that can incorporate plays from any other system, including the wing-T, the veer, the bunch, or the spread offense.
- A system that features fully developed, sequential play packages.
- A system that is capable of employing an enormous amount of misdirection, even more misdirection than the wing-T.
- A system that is not inherently a run offense or a pass offense.
- A system that easily adapts to any type of personnel.
- A system that is extremely effective versus the modern 3-3-5 defense.

What's in this Book for You?

The overall purpose of this book is to provide a comprehensive game plan that exploits the weakness of the 3-3-5 with the I offense. Specifically, the reader will find:

- All of the techniques and assignments to install five fully developed, sequential run/play-action pass series that emphasize quickness, power, and deception.
- Eleven ways to enhance the efficiency of your run offense.

- Seventeen ways to enhance the efficiency of your pass offense
- A comprehensive assortment of I formations that allow an I offense to force the 3-3-5 to defend more gaps than it is capable of defending, reduce the number defenders aligned in the box, dictate secondary coverages, or force 3-3-5 out of its base alignment.
- All of the techniques and assignments necessary install a potent three-, five-, and seven-step dropback passing game versus 3-3-5 pass coverages.
- An explosive assortment of draw, screen, and shovel pass plays that create havoc for the 3-3-5.
- Over 140 I formation plays, organized in an accessible, easy to use and understand playbook format.

Part 1:
Getting Started

1

Overview of the 3-3-5

The 3-3-5 defense is a modern version of the very old 5-3-3 defense. Different forms of the 5-3-3 have emerged, disappeared, and reemerged during the past eighty years. During the 1930s, the 5-3-3 was the standard defense in professional football. During the 1940s it became almost non-existent in the pro game and remained that way until the early 1970s when Hank Stram stacked all three linebackers and replaced the two 5-3 ends with a fourth linebacker and another defensive back. Stram's Kansas City triple stack is very similar to the modern 3-3-5, but because so many offenses now employ spread formations that feature 10, 20, 11, 12, or zero personnel, many coaches have replaced the fourth (outside) linebacker with a fifth defensive back (Note: The author uses a two-digit numbering system to designate personnel type. The first digit indicates the number of running backs in the backfield, and the second digit indicates the number of tight ends. Thus, if the offense were to line up in a standard pro formation that employed two running backs, one tight end, and two wide receivers, the personnel designation would be 21. If a team were to employ four wide receivers and only one running back, the personnel designation would be 10.)

Understanding the Base Defense

Before mentioning any of the variations of the modern 3-3-5, it is important to understand the alignment that has commonly been accepted as the base alignment.

With no universal alignment numbering system, it is first necessary to set one in place. Diagram 1-1 illustrates a fairly common system that the author will use to explain the 3-3-5 base.

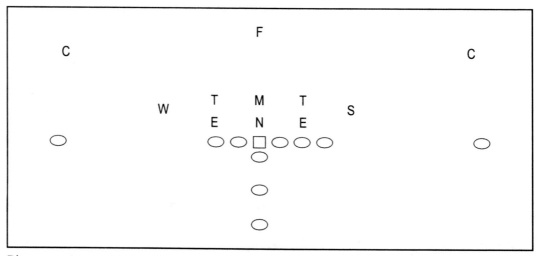

Diagram 1-1

Most teams that employ the modern 3-3-5 will utilize the alignment illustrated in Diagram 1-2 as their base. The following is an overview of the basic responsibilities for each position.

Diagram 1-2

Stud

This player is either a linebacker or a fifth defensive back. All 3-3-5 teams strive to find a hybrid who can not only defeat the block of a big tight end or fullback and effectively shut down an opponent's power running game, but also leave the box and cover a swift wide receiver. Teams that are unable to find a hybrid must either make personnel substitutions or render themselves vulnerable to Stud's weakness. Stud will normally line up in a loose 8 technique and is responsible for primary containment.

Strong and Weak End

Most 3-3-5 teams will align their ends in a 4 technique. From this alignment, the end will usually slant into the B or C gap, employ a two-gap technique (be responsible for both the B and C gap), employ an inside leverage technique (player will step with his outside foot and be responsible for the B gap), or employ an outside leverage technique (player will step with his inside foot and be responsible for the C gap). 3-3-5 teams look for ends who are strong, physical players, capable of pressuring and containing the quarterback.

Nose

The nose plays a 0 technique. He will be asked to control both A gaps, or he will slant into a specific gap. The defense will seek a nose who is physical enough to hold his ground and not get driven backwards. The nose will also be able to control the center and thereby prevent the center from working to the second level (scoop or zone blocking scheme) and blocking Mike.

Whip

This player is primarily a defensive back. He will line up opposite Stud. He is the one who will most frequently make the adjustment of covering an extra wide receiver when man coverage is employed. Because he is primarily a defensive back, he is at a disadvantage versus any offensive set that employs two tight ends. If a linebacker is not substituted for Whip versus 22 and 21 personnel, the defense will be vulnerable. Like Stud, Whip is responsible for primary containment versus run.

Mike

This defender is usually the toughest, most physical linebacker. He will line up directly behind the nose. He is usually responsible for plugging the B gaps versus run.

Strong and Weak Tandems

These players will stack behind the ends. The tandems are responsible for securing the B gaps when the end is responsible for the C gap, and vice versa. Some coaches will have the ends and tandems employ a tango technique (especially versus the option). When a tango technique is employed, the tandem will line up inside shade of the offensive tackle and read the guard-tackle-near back triangle, and the end will line up in a 5 technique and read the tackle. When employing the tango technique, the tandem will plug the B gap when the offensive tackle blocks the defensive end, and the defensive end will secure the C gap. If the offensive tackle blocks inside, the tandem will scrape to the C gap, and the defensive end will close inside and secure the B gap.

Free Safety

When the ball is in the middle of the field, this defender will usually line up eight to 12 yards deep in the center of the offensive formation. When the ball is on the hashes, he will probably favor the wideside of the field but will seldom move outside of the offensive tackle. Versus pass, the free safety will usually cover center field. Versus run, he is usually responsible for providing alley support.

Field Corner

Many 3-3-5 teams flip-flop their cornerbacks. Teams that do this will designate one cornerback as the field corner and the other as the boundary corner. The field corner is the team's best cover player, and he is responsible for covering the #1 receiver aligned toward the wideside of the field, with no help from the free safety. When the ball is in the middle of the field, he will cover his opponent's best receiver.

Boundary Corner

He will line up to the shortside of the field and cover #1. This player will usually receive help from the free safety. He is usually the second-best coverage player on the defense. Oftentimes, the boundary corner will use a jam-and-funnel technique rather than a backpedal technique.

Understanding Variations of the Base

Although many possible variations of the 3-3-5 can be used, Diagrams 1-3A through 1-3D illustrate the four variations that seem to be the most popular.

Diagram 1-3A illustrates a four-deep version in which Whip has moved to the a safety position, the ends have moved to 5 techniques, the tandems are shading the inside eyes of the tackles, and Stud has moved to a 9 technique. This variation enables the defense to employ and disguise a wider variety of secondary coverages and also have the ends and tandems employ a tango technique.

Diagram 1-3B illustrates a three-deep version in which the nose has slid to a strongside 1 technique and Mike has stacked behind him. The strong end has moved to a 7 technique, and the strong tandem has moved to the inside eye of the tight end. On the weakside, the end has moved to a 3 technique, the weak tandem has moved to a 7 technique, and Whip is playing head up with the offensive tackle. Teams that employ this variation usually do so for the purpose of fortifying the strongside of their defense.

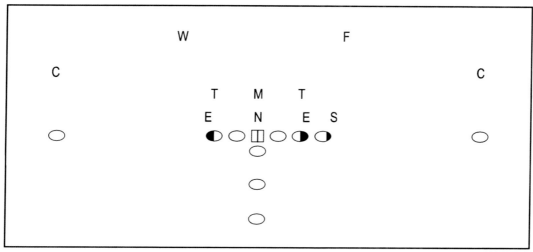

Diagram 1-3A

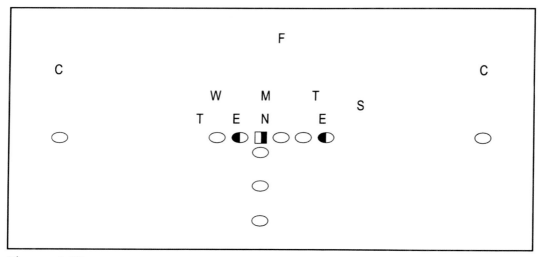

Diagram 1-3B

Although the variation in Diagram 1-3C is illustrated with a three-deep secondary, it is also often used with a four-deep look. This variation is a fairly common one in which the ends move to 4i alignments and the tandems move to the outside eyes of the offensive tackles. When this variation is used, Stud will usually play a 9 technique, and Whip will play a 7 technique.

The last variation is to slide the entire defense to a version of the 3-4 defense. Of course, many different versions of the 3-4 can be used. Diagram 1-3D illustrates the standard version. This variation is often used to make difficult adjustments to certain

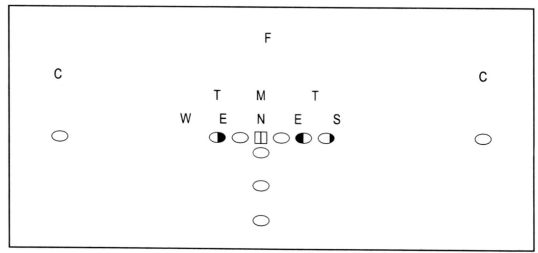

Diagram 1-3C

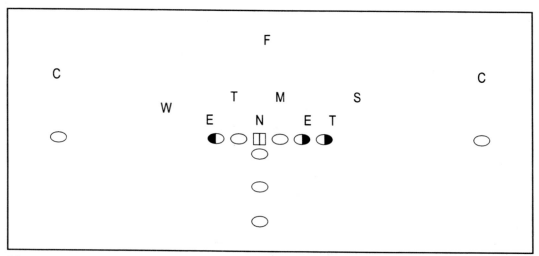

Diagram 1-3D

aceback and empty formations, and also to provide the defense with a wider range of secondary coverages and disguises.

Understanding 3-3-5 Stunt Tactics

A 3-3-5 team may use as many as 12 different stunt tactics in an attempt to pressure the quarterback and disrupt the running game. This section outlines some of the more common tactics employed.

Illusion Blitzes

This tactic involves a six-man pass rush. At the snap of the ball, seven or eight defenders will attack the line of scrimmage. Versus run, these seven or eight defenders will attempt to penetrate the gaps, control the line of scrimmage, force the ballcarrier out of his intended course, and ultimately stop the play in the backfield. Versus pass, six of these defenders will continue to rush the quarterback and the remaining one or two fake pass rushers will "spy" the running backs. This tactic is primarily used on a passing down. Its purpose is to hold the offense accountable for blocking all eight of the defenders aligned in the box and thereby limit the number of receivers an offense can put into pass pattern and safely protect its quarterback. Diagram 1-4 shows an example of an illusion blitz that has the ends spying the running backs.

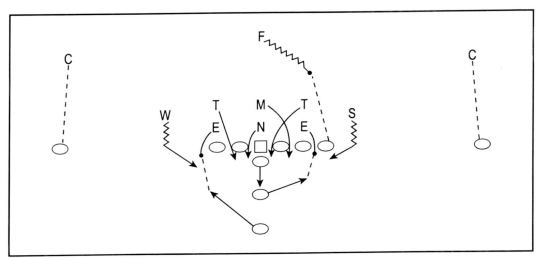

Diagram 1-4

Blitzes

A blitz is similar to an illusion blitz in that it involves a six-man pass rush. Most coaches use a blitz on running downs to pressure the offense from the edge and free up two inside linebackers so that they can pursue the ballcarrier from an inside-out position. Diagram 1-5 illustrates a blitz that sends Stud, Whip, and Mike and frees up the two tandems to pursue run.

Illusion Dogs

The term "dog" refers to a stunt that employs a five-man pass rush. Illusion dogs are almost identical to illusion blitzes. The two differences between these two tactics are that illusion dogs employ five-man pass rushes whereas illusion blitzes employ six-man pass rushes,

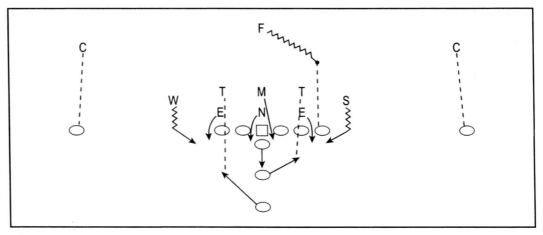

Diagram 1-5

and that cover 1 is usually used with illusion dogs while zero coverage is always used with illusion blitzes. Although illusion dogs put less pressure on a quarterback, many coaches feel more secure using them because their defense is afforded the luxury of a free safety who is backing up the defenders in the box and playing center field versus the pass. Diagram 1-6 shows an example of an illusion dog in which the ends are spying the running backs.

Dogs

Dogs and blitzes are similar and different in the same manner as illusion dogs and illusion blitzes are. Diagram 1-7 shows an example of a dog that sends Mike and Whip and leaves both tandems free to pursue run.

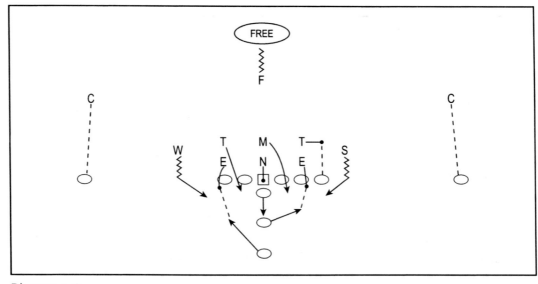

Diagram 1-6

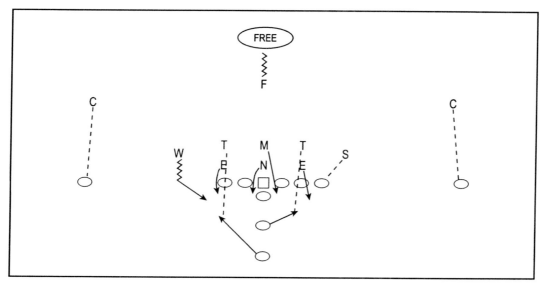

Diagram 1-7

Fire Zone Blitzes

Fire zone blitzes are not really blitzes; they're dogs because they involve five-man pass rushes, and they're used with cover 1. However, the term fire zone blitz has become the universal term used to characterize this tactic. A fire zone blitz is a variation of an illusion dog. Unlike illusion dogs, which have a specific defender cover the tight end and two defenders spy the running backs, fire zone blitzes have three defenders drop off into the under coverage and combo cover the tight end and two running backs. The areas that these three defenders drop off into are referred to as Abel, Baker, and Charlie. In addition to the all of the advantages gained by illusion blitzes and dogs, fire zone blitzes often cause the quarterback to quickly dump the ball off to hot receiver in a long passing situation. This approach frequently results in an offensive failure to gain a first down. Diagram 1-8 shows an example of a common fire zone blitz that has Stud, Mike and the weak end dropping into coverage.

Hybrid Fire Zone Blitzes

This tactic combines a strongside fire zone concept with a weakside illusion. Diagram 1-9 shows a hybrid fire zone blitz in which Stud and the strong tandem are dropping off into coverage and combo-covering the tight end and fullback (similar to a fire zone Abel-Baker drop) and the weak end is spying the tailback.

Old School Zone Blitzes

This tactic involves blitzing linebackers and dropping defensive linemen into a zone coverage. The primary difference between this tactic and the fire zone blitz is the pass coverage. Diagram 1-10 shows an old school zone blitz in which the nose is dropping hook-curl in the under coverage of a three-deep-four-under zone.

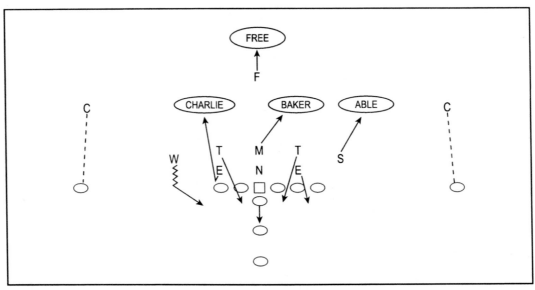

Diagram 1-8

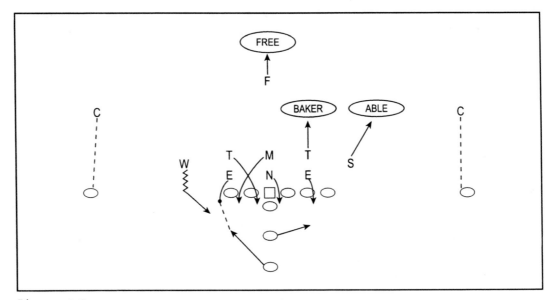

Diagram 1-9

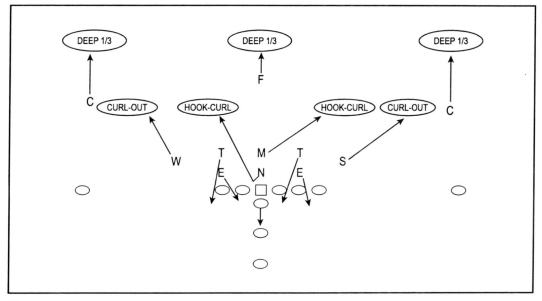

Diagram 1-10

Overloads

Overloads attempt to get more pass rushers on one side of the ball than available pass blockers. Both strongside and weakside overloads are easily attainable using the 3-5 by having a defensive lineman or linebacker employ a delayed pass rush. Diagram 1-11 shows a weakside overload that is created by a delayed pass rush by Mike. This delayed rush by Mike puts the defense in the dilemma of trying to block four pass rushers (illusion of five) with three pass blockers.

Twin Stunts

Twin stunts involve sending two defenders through the same gap. Diagram 1-12 illustrates a twin stunt that is achieved by having the strong end slant into the B gap as the ball is snapped and then having the nose slant behind the end as the nose recognizes pass.

Line Twists

Line twists have always been an effective weapon versus both pass and run. Line twists can occur as the ball is being snapped, or they can be implemented as delayed reactions to pass. Diagram 1-13 shows a line twist that is occurring as the ball is being snapped. This line twist is being used in conjunction with cover 3.

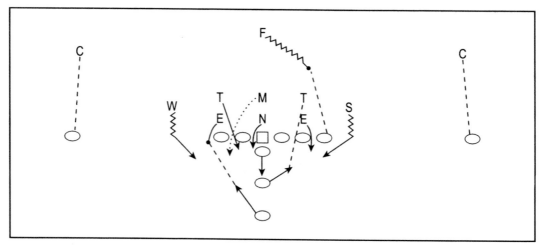

Diagram 1-11

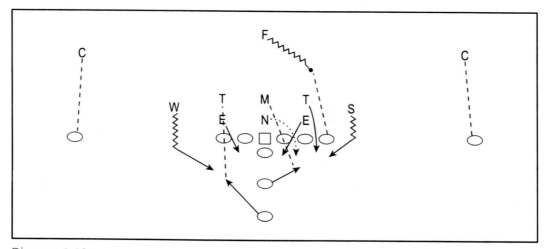

Diagram 1-12

Secondary Blitzes

Secondary blitzes and fake secondary blitzes have always been powerful weapons versus the pass. Diagram 1-14 shows a free safety blitz that is being incorporated into an illusion blitz scheme that gives the offense the impression that the defense is "sending the house."

Understanding 3-3-5 Pass Coverages

Diagrams 1-15A through 1-15G illustrate the seven most commonly used 3-3-5 pass coverages that give the quarterback a three-deep, pre-snap look.

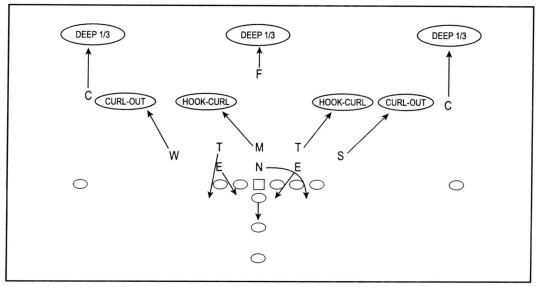

Diagram 1-13

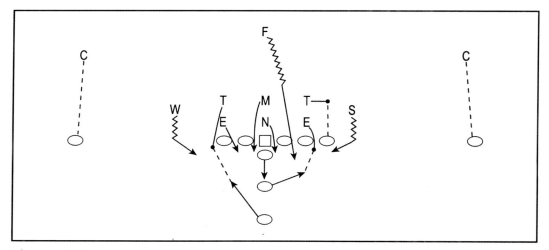

Diagram 1-14

Diagram 1-15A illustrates cover 1, which is probably the most common 3-3-5 coverage. From this coverage, the defense is most likely to employ a dog, an illusion dog, a fire zone blitz, or a robber concept in which four defenders pass rush and one defender drops into the hole to rob crossing patterns. Teams that employ this coverage often try to disrupt the timing of pass routes by having both the boundary corner and Stud employ a jam technique. The advantage of the coverage is that it provides the defense with a free safety who can play center field versus pass and provide alley support versus run.

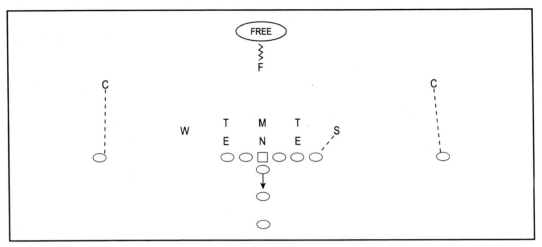

Diagram 1-15A

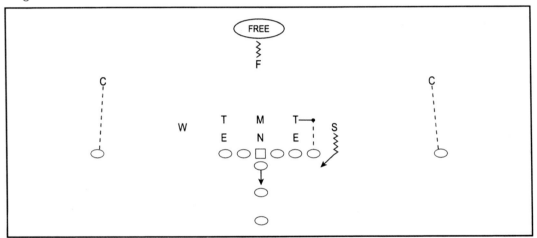

Diagram 1-15B

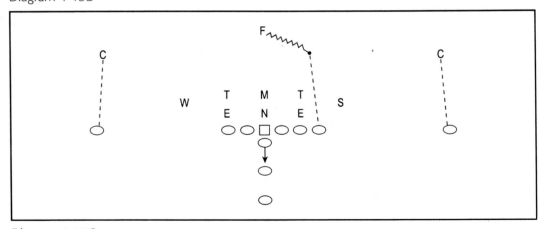

Diagram 1-15C

Diagram 1-15B illustrates a variation of cover 1 in which the strong tandem covers the tight end and Stud rushes from the edge. Teams often employ this variation in an attempt to stop strongside sweeps.

Diagram 1-15C illustrates zero coverage that has been disguised as cover 1. Teams use this coverage to pressure the offense with blitzes and illusion blitzes. The strength of zero coverage is that it affords the defense a six-man pass rush. Its weakness is that the defense is left without a free safety and if a run breaks the line of scrimmage (or a receiver gets behind a pass defender), the possibility of a touchdown is greatly increased. Another weakness is that it often leaves the defense vulnerable to screen passes.

Diagrams 1-15D and 1-15E illustrate two variations of zero coverage that are used for the purpose of achieving either a strongside or weakside overload.

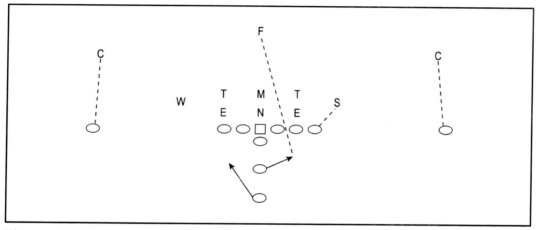

Diagram 1-15D

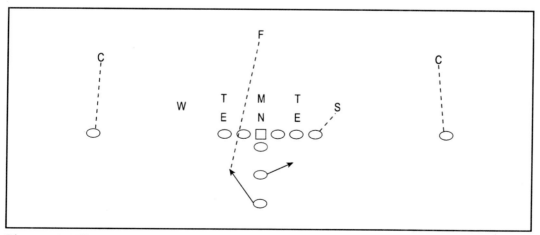

Diagram 1-15E

Diagram 1-15F illustrates a four-under-three-deep zone, and Diagram 1-15G shows a five-under-three-deep zone. The defense is most likely to use line twists and old school zone blitzes with this coverage. The strength of either zone coverage is that all of the defenders are keying the ball. Consequently, more interceptions usually result. Its weaknesses are that the number of pass rushers has been decreased, the offense can flood the zones, the zones can be stretched both vertically and horizontally, and the pass rush is susceptible to draws and shovel passes.

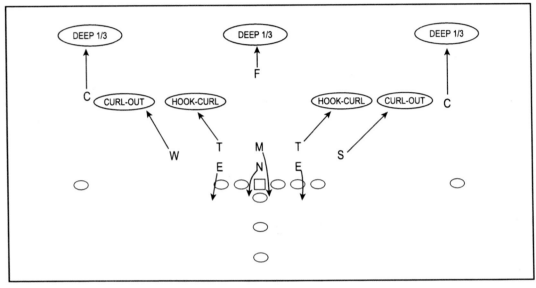

Diagram 1-15F

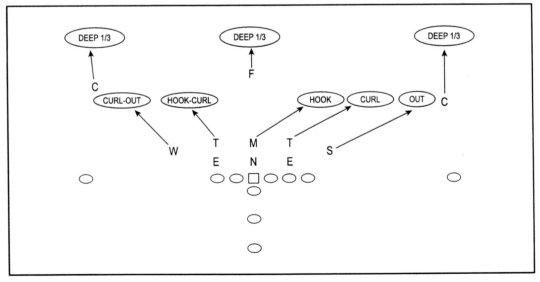

Diagram 1-15G

Diagrams 1-16A through 1-16E illustrate five additional coverages that can be added to the 3-3-5 repertoire from a four-deep look. It should first be noted, however, that all of the coverages that were illustrated for three-deep looks can also be employed with four-deep looks.

Diagram 1-16A illustrates cover 2 man, the purpose of which is to jam the wide receivers, disrupt the timing of their pass routes, and deny them short patterns. Its weaknesses are that it is not strong against the run, only six defenders are left in the box when one of the running backs go into motion, it only provides the defense with a four-man pass rush, and it limits a defense in the types of stunt tactics that it might employ.

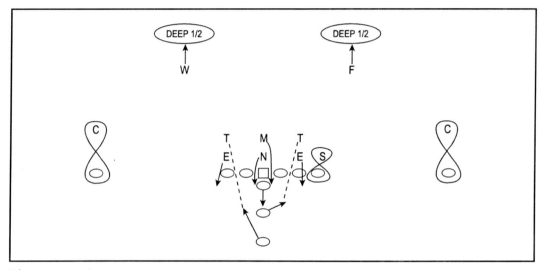

Diagram 1-16A

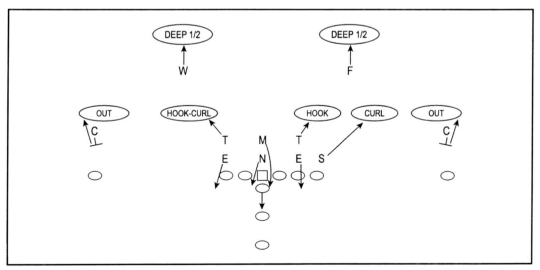

Diagram 1-16B

Diagram 1-16B illustrates cover 2 zone coverage. This coverage is stronger versus the run than cover 2 man. Although it usually does an excellent job of disrupting the wide receivers and denying them the quick out, hitch, and slant, it does have all of the other weaknesses of any zone coverage. Furthermore, it only provides the defense with a four-man pass rush and limits its stunt capabilities.

Diagrams 1-16 C and 1-16D illustrate two variations of cover 3, cover 3 cloud, and cover 3 sky. These two variations have all of the strengths and weaknesses as those mentioned in the three-deep variation of cover 3.

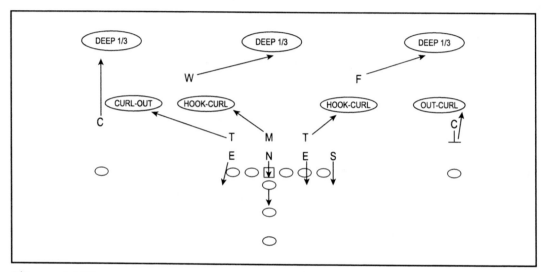

Diagram 1-16C

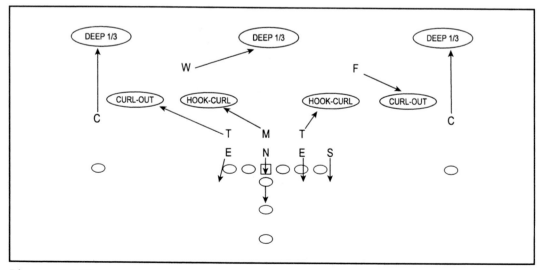

Diagram 1-16D

Diagram 1-16E illustrates quarter-halves coverage, a combination coverage in which cover 2 zone is played toward the weakside of the formation, and quarters coverage is being played toward the strongside. The purpose of quarters coverage is to have the free safety take away the flanker's post or curl patterns. Sometimes a defense will employ quarters coverage on both sides of the ball.

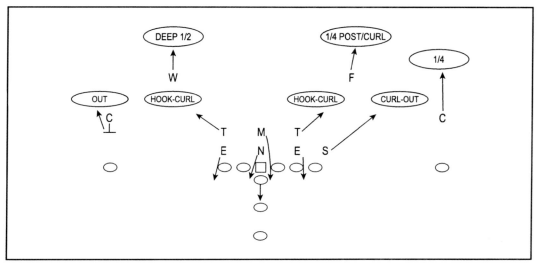

Diagram 1-16E

Strengths of the 3-3-5

- It is new and many coaches aren't really sure how to block it and effectively game plan against it.

- It is extremely flexible. Nickel-dime substitutions can easily be made without disrupting the overall scheme, which enables the defense to automatically adapt itself to any type of offensive personnel that is on the field.

- The defense is an eight-man front, which gives it an advantage against the run. Despite this strength, the defense always has four or five defensive backs on the field, which also makes it a great pass defense.

- The triple stack frequently results in one of the stacked linebackers ending up unblocked.

- The tango technique can help the defense become sound versus the option.

- Pass coverages are easily disguised and can be employed from both a three-deep and four-deep look.

- The defense is conducive to multiple coverages.

- Explosive stunt packages can easily be installed into the system.

Weaknesses of the 3-3-5

- Many 3-3-5 teams have not evolved into exact, well-defined option rules.
- The defense becomes vulnerable to sweep plays when the tandems blitz and do not gain enough penetration to stop the play in the backfield or bounce the ballcarrier deep and wide.
- Seldom do teams have a hybrid Stud. Such teams often do not have the sophistication to make adequate personnel substitutions.
- Outside plays that are initiated by an inside fake often freeze the tandems and either slow or nullify their pursuit.
- Because most 3-3-5 teams rely heavily upon the blitz, their defensive backs are often put in one-on-one situations that sometimes result in mismatches.
- Because most 3-3-5 teams rely heavily upon the blitz, they are frequently susceptible to screen passes.
- Formations that employ two tight ends place Whip (who is primarily a defensive back) at a disadvantage and prevent the defense from employing four-deep secondaries.
- A trey formation, a variation of trips with two tight ends and two wide, often forces the defense out of its 3-3-5 base.
- A double tight end bunch formation forces the defense to defend 10 gaps with eight defenders.
- Tight wing and slot formations force Stud out of his normal alignment.
- A nasty split by the tight end can force Stud to move to a position that makes him inept at helping stop inside plays.
- A twin formation usually results in Whip having to leave the box.
- The defense is often susceptible to picks and rubs because it relies heavily on man coverage.
- The loose 8 technique employed by Stud enables a tight end to release easily inside and block either the strong end or tandem.
- Although the defense is great against the spread offense, it often has difficulty adapting to the power game if proper adjustments are not made.

2

Eleven Ways to Enhance the Efficiency of Your Run Offense

Offensive coaches are continually searching for ways to manipulate a defense, and defensive coaches are constantly searching for ways to counter these tactics. The purpose of this chapter is present eleven tactics that will help I formation coaches gain an edge in their running game.

#1: Organize Plays into Sequential Play Packages

The difference between a bunch of plays and a real offense is sequential play packaging. Sequential play packaging groups plays into a series. When the ball is hiked, each play in a series initially looks like every other play in the series. Because a complete package is capable of attacking all sectors of a defense (the inside sector, the off-tackle hole, the perimeter, and the secondary), sequential play packaging causes defensive uncertainty, inhibits defensive play recognition, slows defensive pursuit, and ultimately abates defensive aggression.

#2: Force Defenders to Play Assignment Football

Forced assignment is directly related to sequential play packaging. A clever defensive coach can flim-flam many modern offenses, but offenses that possess fully developed play packages are capable of controlling what a defense can and cannot do. This capability is referred to as forced assignment football. Fully developed play packages hold defensive coaches accountable for devising game plans that adequately stop each and every play in the series. They also force defenders to thoroughly check their specific assignment before pursuing other plays within the series.

#3: Double-Bind Defenders

The double bind puts a defender in a no-win, "damned if he does, damned if he doesn't" dilemma. For example, if the 3-3-5 Stud linebacker is coached to tighten to a 9 technique versus a wing formation, he is probably also taught to close inside and seal the C gap whenever the tight end blocks inside. If the defender reacts properly to his key, he immediately becomes vulnerable to a crack block by the wingback and is therefore unable to stop the tailback bounce (Diagram 2-1A). On the other hand, if the wingback is *influencing* Stud and has no intent to block the defender, Stud becomes vulnerable to the off-tackle play (Diagram 2-1B). Double binding can be applied to almost any defender aligned in the box.

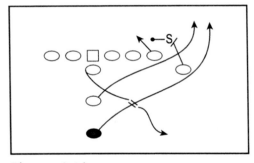
Diagram 2-1A

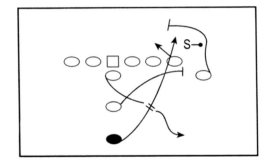
Diagram 2-1B

#4: Double-Cross Defenders

The tactic of double-crossing defenders is also referred to as false keying. Almost all coaches teach defenders to read and react to specific keys. Keys are intended to be road maps that lead defenders to the ball. Coaches can destroy a defender's mental confidence in his keys by employing offensive tactics that are contrary to the defender's keys. Diagram 2-2 illustrates a play in which the right side of the line is employing a base-blocking scheme and the left side of the line is employing a G-kick-iso scheme. It is impossible to for the defenders aligned in the box to arrive at valid keys that will lead them to the ball when confronted by this type of blocking scheme conjoined with the illustrated backfield action. Because the ball can be given to either the tailback or the wingback, defenders on both sides of center must stay at home. Obviously a nose tackle, playing a 0 technique, would really be put in a bind in this situation. Double crossing greatly assists the offense in reducing defensive aggressiveness and pursuit.

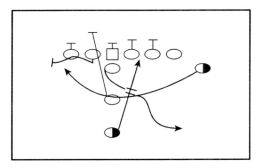

Diagram 2-2

#5: Employ Real Misdirection

Misdirection is one of the most potent offensive weapons in football. It is also a frequently neglected aspect of many modern offenses. Misdirection not only creates confusion, it abates defensive aggressiveness. Having a tailback step right before he runs left is not misdirection. Misdirection occurs when the defense, the referees, the cameramen, and the fans are all trying to figure out who's got the ball.

#6: Increase the Number of Gaps a Defense Must Defend

Defenses are accustomed to defending eight gaps (four gaps on each side of center). By incorporating bunch formations that utilize I formation principles, an offense can increase the number of gaps that a defense must defend. The bunch formation illustrated in Diagram 2-3 forces a defense to defend ten gaps.

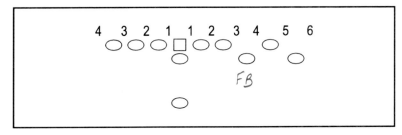

Diagram 2-3

#7: Reduce the Number of Defenders in the Box with a Twins Formation

This formation is great to use versus an eight-man front that plays a lot of cover 3 because it leaves the defense with only seven players in the box (Diagram 2-4A). If the defense insists upon keeping eight players in the box by playing zero coverage (Diagram 2-4B), the offense has two one-on-one situations with its two wide receivers. If the offense attempts to keep eight in the box by playing a zero/corners-over coverage, it not only has two one-on-one situations, but is has also drastically weakened itself to runs directed toward the tight end (Diagram 2-4C).

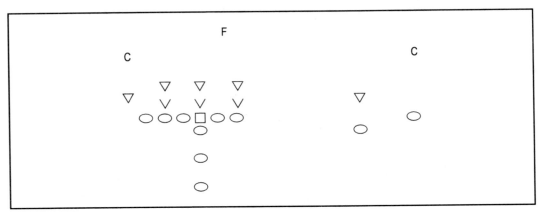

Diagram 2-4A

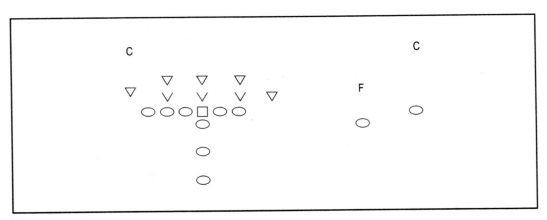

Diagram 2-4B

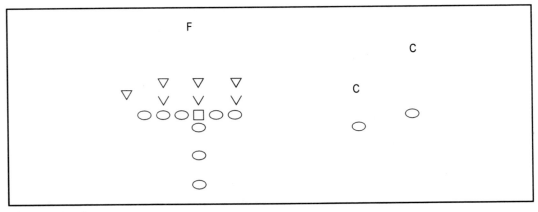

Diagram 2-4C

#8: Reduce the Number of Defenders in the Box with a Nasty Split

By splitting one's tight end two-and-a-half to four yards from the offensive tackle, the primary force player in the 3-3-5 is forced with the dilemma of either maintaining outside leverage and leaving only six players in the box (Diagram 2-5A), or relinquishing outside leverage and becoming susceptible to the quick pitch (Diagram 2-5B).

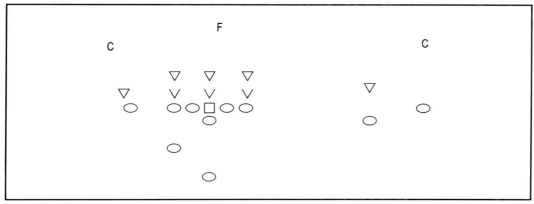

Diagram 2-5A

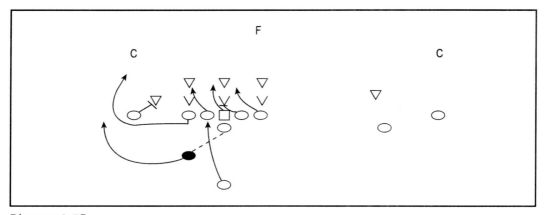

Diagram 2-5B

#9: Shift from End over to Trips and Vice Versa

By putting both wide receivers on the same side of the ball and one's fullback in a slotback position, an I offense can beguile an eight-man front. Because either the fullback or tight end can be sent into motion, the formation has little effect upon the running game. The formation does, however, force most defensive coordinators to get out of their base by moving a linebacker out of the box. Diagram 2-6A illustrates how this tactic reduces the 3-3-5 to a 3-4. If the defense refuses to adjust (because the #2 receiver is ineligible), the offense can immediately exploit the coverage and create a trips formation by moving the tight end on the line and the #2 receiver off the line (Diagram 2-6B). Offensive coordinators can have a lot of fun playing mind games with the defense by shifting the two formations back and forth a couple of times before the ball is snapped.

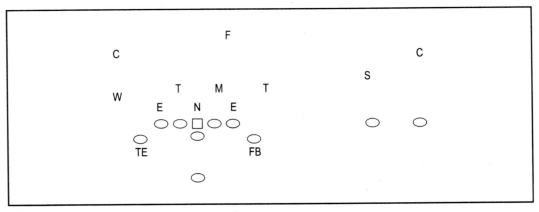

Diagram 2-6A

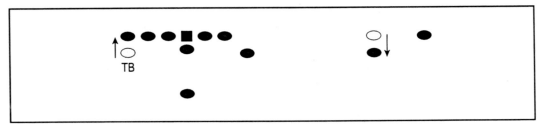

Diagram 2-6B

#10: Option a Great Defense Instead of Blocking It

Both Bob Ladouceur and J.T. Curtis have produced unbelievable winning records by optioning rather than blocking some of the finest defenses in America. The success that these two coaches have achieved with the option speaks louder than all of the words that have ever been spoken or written about football strategy.

#11: Double-team a Tango Linebacker

For many years, defenses have successfully defended the option by using a tango technique. When this technique is employed, two defenders will read a single blocker and vary their option assignments based upon this blocker's movements. Eight-man fronts, such as the 3-3-5, must employ this technique to successfully defend the option. A 3-3-5 team will often have the end and tandem linebacker read the offensive tackle (Stud will be assigned pitch). In Diagram 2-7A the offensive tackle blocks the end. Versus this scheme, the tandem linebacker will attack the dive and the end will play the quarterback. In Diagram 2-7B, the offensive tackle blocks inside. Versus this scheme, the end will attack the dive and the tandem linebacker will scrape to quarterback, but because the tight end is also blocking the tandem linebacker, Stud is left in a two-on-one dilemma of trying to stop both the quarterback and pitch.

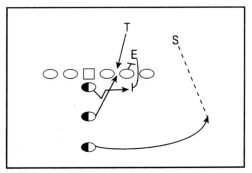

Diagram 2-7A

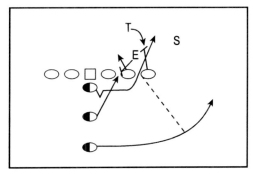

Diagram 2-7B

3

Manipulating the 3-3-5 with Multiple I Formations

The most important goal of any offensive is defensive manipulation. In the introduction, the versatility of the I formation was discussed. The following are additional advantages of the I:

- A team's best running back is aligned in the middle of the formation; therefore, he can hit all holes on both sides of center with equal effectiveness.

- It is a quick-hitting offense.

- Both power and deception can be incorporated with equal effectiveness.

- It is equally effective as a "middle of the field" or "red zone" offense.

- Because the I backfield adapts to a vast variety of receiver sets, formations can be used to limit stunt capability and manipulate fronts and coverages.

- Because the offense reverses cycles, it is a natural antidote for the many defensive tactics that have been developed to defense the spread.

The I offense doesn't necessitate that the fullback lines up directly in front of the tailback (Diagram 3-1A). Although this alignment is the traditional version that Tom Nugent developed in the 1950s, other variations have evolved. The variations of offset I, which most coaches refer to as king (Diagram 3-1B) and queen (Diagram 3-1C), are evolutions that have become popular during the last decade. A number of NFL teams have also developed a full house I (Diagram 3-1D) in recent years. Setting the fullback in a slot or wing position and calling him an H back (Diagram 3-1E) dates back at least twenty years. Of course, the power I (Diagrams 3-1F and 3-1G) is at least fifty years old.

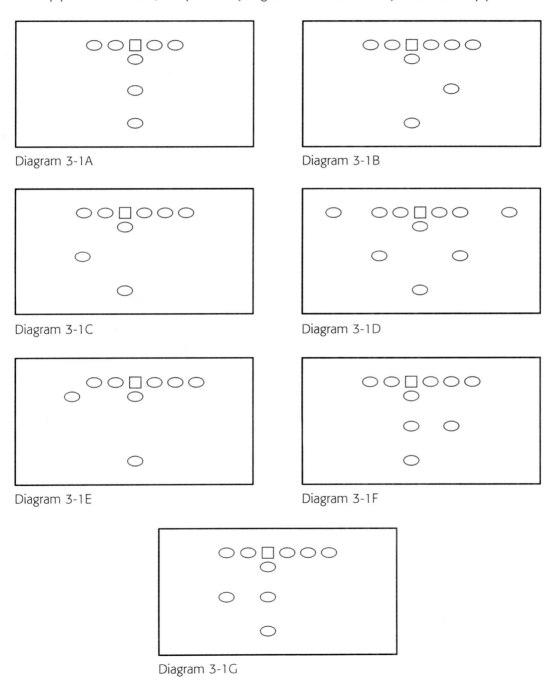

Diagram 3-1A

Diagram 3-1B

Diagram 3-1C

Diagram 3-1D

Diagram 3-1E

Diagram 3-1F

Diagram 3-1G

The remainder of this chapter will be devoted to considering the strengths and weaknesses of various I formations and discussing the possible ways that these formations can be used to manipulate the 3-3-5 defense.

Pro Right (Diagram 3-2)

Quicks

The advantage of the pro right formation is that it enables the defense to stretch the field horizontally. It can be used on the hash or in the middle of the field. It is a good formation to throw a quick pass in which the quarterback takes three or less steps. When the free safety is in the middle of the formation, it is also a good formation to throw passes that require the quarterback to take five or seven steps. When the free safety lines up in a position that will enable him to cover the tight end, the defense is capable of achieving a strongside overload pass rush, which necessitate adjustments in pass protection and/or hot reads. It is a decent formation to run out of, but not a great one, because the defense is only required to defend seven gaps. Also, misdirection is limited.

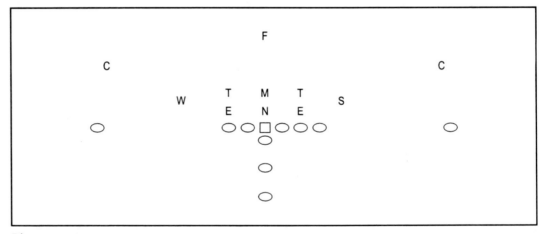

Diagram 3-2

Tite Right (Diagram 3-3)

BALL
ON
HASH
2-WING

Due to the presence of only one wide receiver, horizontal stretch of the field is limited. It is best to use this formation when the ball is on the hash. To obtain maximum stretch of the field with this formation, the flanker should be aligned toward the wideside, never into the boundary. The addition of an extra tight end forces the defense to defend all eight of the gaps. Otherwise, this formation is identical to pro.

Wing Right (Diagram 3-4)

This run formation is a great way to force the defense to defend nine gaps. It is also a great play-action pass formation. The formation has great misdirection possibilities. The tight wing requires Stud to adjust his alignment. Stud cannot possibly play a loose 8 technique versus this formation and be effective at stopping off-tackle plays. The wingback can be used as a ballcarrier, a blocker, a pass receiver, or as the force that double binds Stud if Stud moves to a 9 technique. It is a good formation in the red zone. The obvious weakness of the formation is that it does not stretch the defense horizontally.

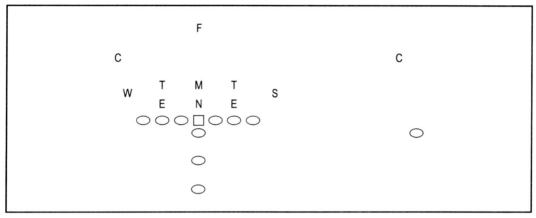

Diagram 3-3

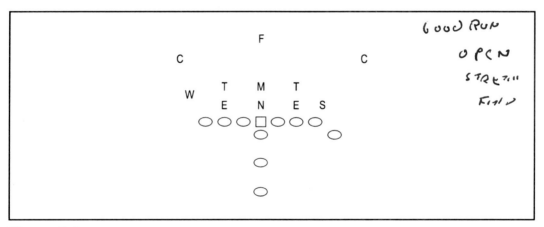

Diagram 3-4

Open Wing Right (Diagram 3-5)

This formation forces the defense to defend eight gaps. The wide receiver helps stretch the defense horizontally if he is aligned to the wideside of the field. Otherwise, the formation is identical to wing right.

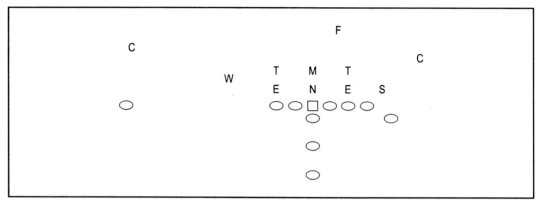

Diagram 3-5

Over Wing Right (Diagram 3-6)

HASH

This formation is good to use when the ball is on the hash. The split end should be aligned toward the wideside of the field. The purpose to the end-over alignment is to remove the corner and soften run support toward the wing. Whip's adjustment is, of course, the primary consideration in attacking the 3-3-5. If both Whip and Stud line up toward the wing, runs away from the wing are good because the defense must use their weak cornerback for primary weakside containment. On the other hand, if Whip remains on the weakside, runs toward the wing should be good plays. Another thing that must be considered is the alignment of the tight end. If the tight end lines up at the left tackle position, he is an eligible pass receiver and it is quite likely that he will get lost in traffic and be wide open on a play-action pass. On the other hand, if he is aligned in his normal position next to the right offensive tackle, neither he nor the left tackle is eligible to receive a pass. Lining up the tight end in the left tackle position and the left tackle in the tight end position may alter each player's blocking assignments slightly and require a little extra coaching, but the advantages are probably worth the effort.

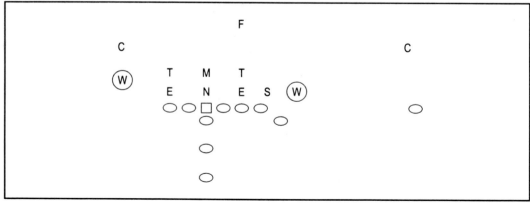

Diagram 3-6

Slice Right (Diagram 3-7)

This formation has the same coaching points as pro regarding passing. However, slice is a better run formation than pro. Misdirection is greatly enhanced by the presence of the slot back. Furthermore, the slot back can be sent into motion as a lead blocker or to create other formations. Also, because a slotback should be much quicker than a tight end this may also be a better pass formation than pro.

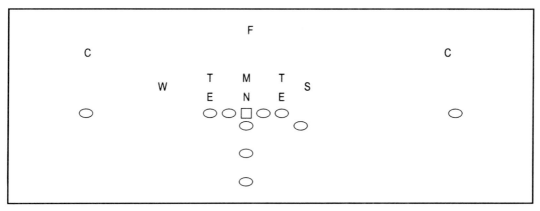

Diagram 3-7

Spread Right (Diagram 3-8)

RUN 2 RTC SIDE

This pass formation is great to use on the hash or in the middle of the field. Most 3-3-5 teams will want to keep their free safety in center field and will therefore walk Whip out to a position that will enable him to cover the slot receiver. Some teams will try to "cheat" by walking Whip halfway between the slot receiver and the offensive tackle. Versus such teams, a play-action fake will freeze Whip and enable the slot receiver to find an open window straight down the field. Because the defense is only required to defend six gaps, this is not a great run formation. Runs toward the two-receiver side are the best choice because Whip will more than likely leave the box.

Twins Right (Diagram 3-9)

klasif

This formation is good to use when the ball is on the hash. Like spread, the formation will usually force Whip to leave the box. It also has the additional advantage of forcing the defense to defend seven gaps. Twins is a good formation from which to throw the bubble screen. Also, because the slot receiver is off the line of scrimmage, it is difficult for Whip to jam this receiver. When the slot receiver lines up on the line of scrimmage and #1 backs off, the formation is called dual right. Tops is a good formation to throw the jailbreak screen.

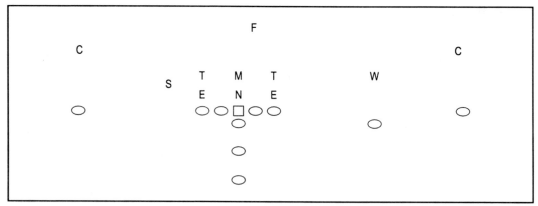

Diagram 3-8

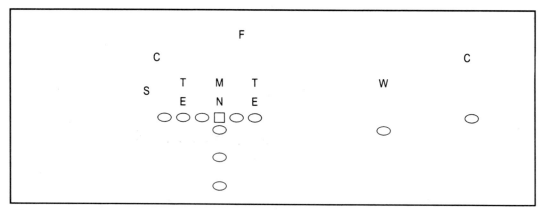

Diagram 3-9

Slash Right (Diagram 3-10)

Woody Hayes used this same formation to win a National Championship in 1968. It is a great run formation because it not only forces the defense to defend 8 gaps, but the presence of the slot back opens the door for a number of potent misdirection plays. The slot back can also be sent into motion to create a twins formation and remove Whip from the box. It is also a good pass formation. When the ball is on the hash, the split end should be aligned toward the wideside of the field in order to attain maximum horizontal stretch of the defense.

Open Slot Right (Diagram 3-11)

This formation double binds Stud's alignment. If Stud lines up inside of the tight end, he is susceptible to a crack block by the tight end. If he lines up outside of the tight end, he opens up a funnel and allows both the tight end and the slotback to crack inside. He is in a no win situation. This formation can be used in the middle of the field or on the hash. When used on the hash, the split end should be aligned to the wideside of the field. Although not illustrated, two other variations are possible with this formation: slot (which uses no split ends) and over slot (in which the split end is aligned on the same side as the slot).

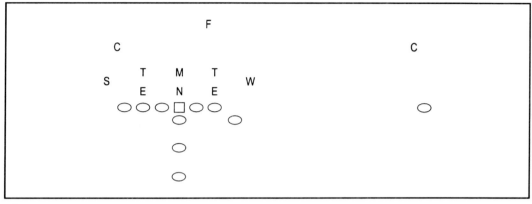

Diagram 3-10

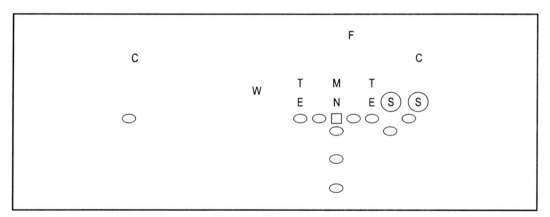

Diagram 3-11

Cluster Right (Diagram 3-12)

This formation is great to use anywhere on the field. It is even being used extensively in the NFL. The formation forces a defense to defend ten gaps and four eligible pass receivers who are aligned on or near the line of scrimmage. Because of alignment of the clustered receivers, they are in an ideal position to create rubs (natural picks), which create havoc for man coverage. This alignment enhances the formation's value in the red zone. Cluster compels a 3-3-5 team to get out of its base. The most common adjustment is the illustrated one. It is up to each coach to determine where he will align his fullback. The fullback can be aligned at the left end position, where he can step off the line and go into motion as blocker or ballcarrier (if this is done either the slotback or wingback must step up onto the line). He can also be aligned at either the slotback or wingback position. Countless possibilities are available. For coaches who wish to explore these possibilities in greater detail, a number of books and videos on this subject are available from Coaches Choice.

Deuce Right (Diagram 3-13)

Deuce right is a good middle-of-the-field pass formation. Although the fullback is aligned in the slotback position and can be sent in motion, the potential of this formation to mount an explosive running attack is limited. The primary strength of the formation is that it enables a quarterback to easily read the alignment of the free safety and direct his passing attack away from potential overload blitz schemes.

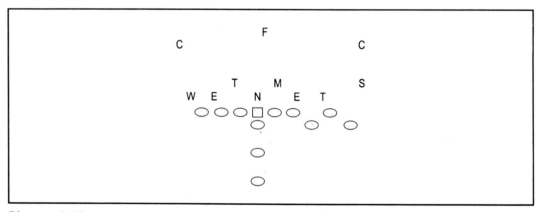

Diagram 3-12

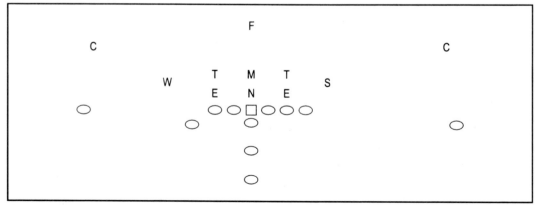

Diagram 3-13

The Trip Family (Diagrams 3-14A through 3-14F)

Diagrams 3-14A through 3-14F illustrate six formations that make up the trip family. These good hash mark formations almost always force the 3-3-5 out of its base alignment. The split end and flanker will be aligned at the #1 and #2 positions in all six formations, but it is up to each coach to determine where he will align the fullback and tight end. Some coaches may prefer to align the tight end in the #3 position and the fullback in the #4 position. Others may prefer the opposite arrangement. The trip family enables the offense to stretch the field horizontally with four eligible receivers who are aligned on or near the line of scrimmage. It also enables the offense to maintain many of its sequential two-back running plays by sending either #3 or #4 into motion. Furthermore, by shifting players on and off the line, the offense can create defensive confusion about which players are eligible pass receivers. The name and coaching point for each formation is as follows:

- **Trips**–(Diagram 3-14A). Provides the offense with four eligible pass receivers on or near the line of scrimmage. #3 can be sent into motion as a blocking back or used for misdirection. Good formation for the bubble screen.

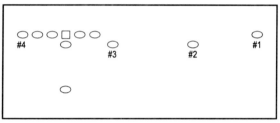

Diagram 3-14A

- **Tops**–(Diagram 3-14B). Same coaching points as trips. Good formation for the jailbreak screen.

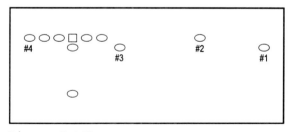

Diagram 3-14B

- **Treez**–(Diagram 3-14C). Good pass formation because it makes it difficult for the defense to jam the two wide receivers. Limits the running game.

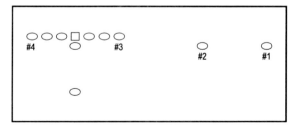

Diagram 3-14C

- **U-Trips**–(Diagram 3-14D). #3 is no longer an eligible pass receiver. #4 can be sent into motion as a blocking back or used for misdirection. Good formation for the bubble screen.

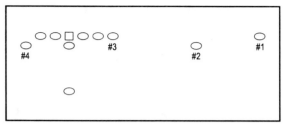

Diagram 3-14D

- **U-Tops**–(Diagram 3-14E). #3 is no longer an eligible pass receiver. #4 can be sent into motion as a blocking back or used for misdirection. Good formation for the jailbreak screen.

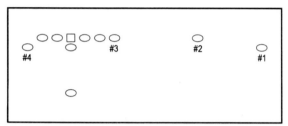

Diagram 3-14E

- **U-Treez**–(Diagram 3-14F). #2 is no longer an eligible pass receiver. Both #3 and #4 can be sent into motion as a blocking back, or either can be used for misdirection. Good formation for the jailbreak screen.

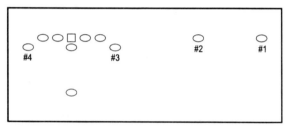

Diagram 3-14F

The Full House I (Diagram 3-15)

The full house I is primarily a red zone formation when both ends are in a tight alignment. When the ends assume a nasty split (as shown in Diagram 3-15), the quick pitch potential of the formation is enhanced. By splitting both ends, as some NFL teams are doing, the formation's pass potential is strengthened, especially when one of the upbacks is sent into motion.

The Power I (Diagram 3-16)

Because the formation can employ two tight ends, two split ends, or one of each type, and also because the halfback can be aligned toward or away from the tight end, many variations of this formation are possible. The basic coaching points, however, are identical to that of the full house I.

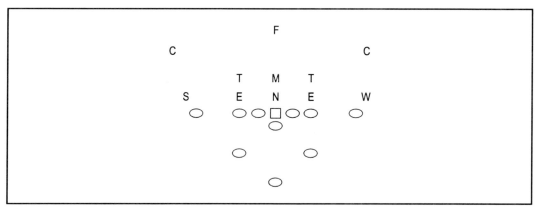

Diagram 3-15

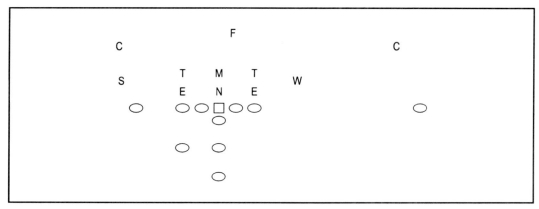

Diagram 3-16

Part 2:
Attacking the 3-3-5 with the Run

Attacking the 3-3-5
with the Power Series

The power series is one of the oldest and most explosive series in football. Its roots go all the way back to the early 1900s when Pop Warner's single wing was overpowering defenses at the point of attack. The series is initiated by attacking the heart of the defense, the off-tackle hole. Although the lead-off play of the series relies on power, its sequential complementary plays enable it to attack all sectors of the defense with finesse and misdirection.

Off-Tackle Power

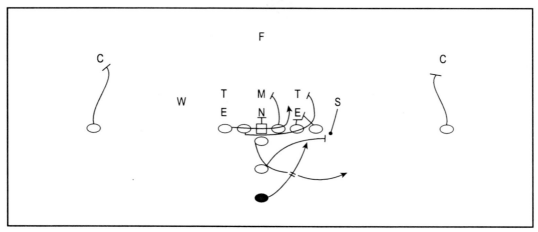

Diagram 4-1

Coaching Points: This play is the trademark play of the series. The offense should become so proficient running this play that the defense must cheat in order to stop it and thus leave itself vulnerable to another play in the series.

Y: Double-teams the defensive end with the AST unless the end slants into the B gap (Y will then work to the second level and block the strong tandem), or the strong tandem blitzes the B gap, in which case Y will then block the defensive end by himself.

AST: Double-teams the defensive end with Y unless the defensive end slants into the B gap (AST will then block the end by himself) or the strong tandem blitzes the B gap, in which case AST will then release pressure from the defensive end and block the strong tandem.

ASG: Blocks Mike. If Mike blitzes weakside, ASG looks first for the weak tandem and then downfield.

C: Steps strongside and blocks the nose.

BSG: Pulls and leads.

BST: Fills and leads through the attackside B gap. Blocks any defensive penetration along the way.

X: Blocks downfield.

QB: Reverse pivots and deals the ball to the tailback as deep as possible. Fakes the quarterback keep. Does not look at the tailback after the handoff. Instead, QB "eyeballs" the free safety to determine if this defender is respecting the quarterback keep.

TB: Steps directly at the hole. Does not look for the ball; it's the quarterback's responsibility to make the handoff. Protects the ball with both hands until he is out of traffic. Runs to daylight.

FB: Steps with his right foot directly toward the outside foot of the ASG. Doing so enables the FB to gain an ideal kick out position on Stud. Blocks Stud at the hip and drives him outside.

Z: Blocks downfield.

Using Formations to Augment the Off-Tackle Power

Employing a wingback greatly enhances the off-tackle play. The presence of a wingback forces the defense to defend five strongside gaps which should result in Stud being forced to move onto the line in either a 9 technique or tight 8 technique. Diagram 4-2 illustrates three examples of how a wingback can be used to intensify the effectiveness of the play. Diagram 4-2A illustrates how the wingback can be used to double bind Stud by attacking Stud's outside shoulder at the snap and threatening to block the defender inside. The wingback then works to the second level and seals off inside pursuit. Diagram 4-2B illustrates how the wingback can be used to create the illusion of misdirection, and Diagram 4-2C shows how the wingback can be used to impair secondary pass/run reads by creating the illusion of play-action pass.

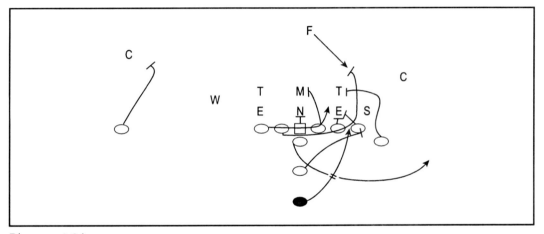

Diagram 4-2A

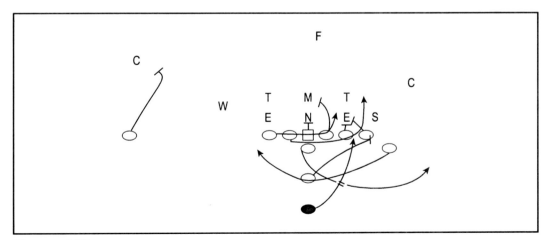

Diagram 4-2B

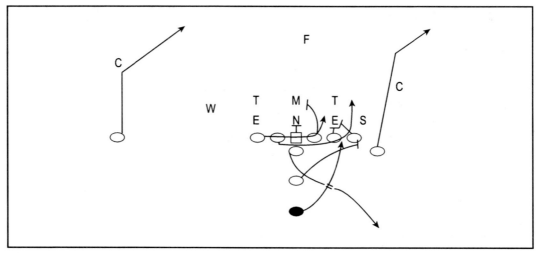

Diagram 4-2C

Diagram 4-3 shows how the play can be augmented by a tight slot formation. Most 3-3-5 teams will align Stud outside of the tight end and thus leave the defense with no defenders aligned in C and D gaps. Diagram 4-4 shows how the offense can increase the effectiveness of the play by employing a twins formation to reduce the 3-3-5 to a seven-man front. Lastly, Diagram 4-5 demonstrates how the effectiveness of the off-tackle power can be intensified by forcing the 3-3-5 out of its base alignment by stemming from trips to a U trips formation.

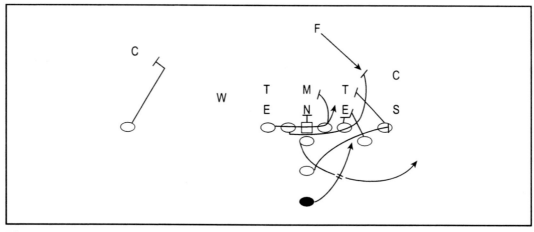

Diagram 4-3

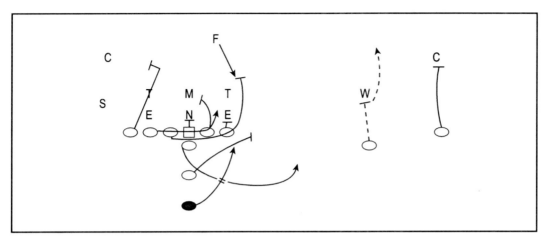

Diagram 4-4

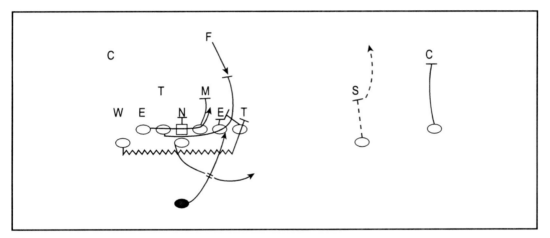

Diagram 4-5

Power Option

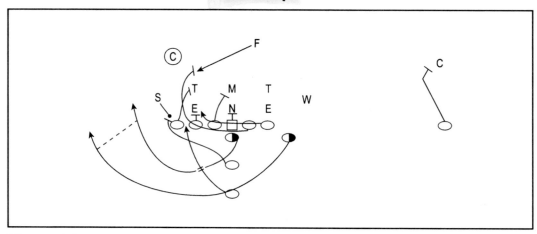

Diagram 4-6

Coaching Points: This play is an effective addition to the series whenever the defense begins to over-play the power. Some slotbacks may have to go into quick motion to establish a proper pitch relationship with the quarterback.

Y: Combo blocks the stack with the AST. Seals the C gap and bumps the defensive end. Works to the second level and blocks the strong tandem unless the strong tandem blitzes the B gap. Y will then block the defensive end by himself.

AST: Combo blocks the stack with Y. Attacks the defensive end and drives him backwards but keeps the strong tandem in his periphery. Continues to block the defensive end unless the strong tandem blitzes the B gap. If this situation occurs, AST will release pressure from the end and block the strong tandem.

ASG: Blocks Mike. If Mike blitzes weak side, ASG looks first for the weak tandem and then downfield.

C: Steps strong and blocks the nose.

BSG: Pulls and blocks the free safety.

BST: Fills and leads through the attackside B gap. Blocks any defensive penetration along the way.

X: Blocks downfield.

QB: Reverse pivots but does not gain as much depth as he normally would on the power. Fakes to the tailback and immediately locates the cornerback. If the cornerback is playing him, the QB will aggressively run at him and force him to defend either the pitch or keep.

TB: Fakes the off-tackle power. A great fake is extremely important; the TB must convince the defense that he has the ball.

FB: Blocks Stud. Attacks Stud's far hip and hooks the defender inside.

SB: Runs an option course behind the quarterback and maintains a proper pitch relationship with quarterback (approximately 3-3).

Power Shovel

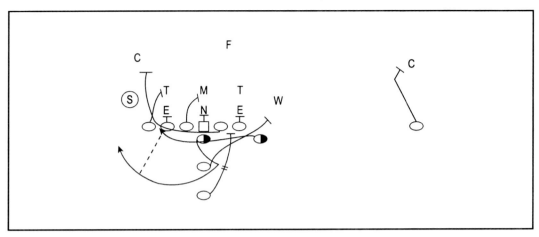

Diagram 4-7

Coaching Points: Not all coaches will choose to run the power by having their quarterback threaten the perimeter after handing the ball to the tailback. Some may prefer to have their quarterback set up to pass; others may elect to have him fake a bootleg. This shovel/option is for those coaches who fancy having their quarterback bootleg.

Y: Combo blocks the stack with the AST. Seals the C gap and bumps the defensive end. Works to the second level and blocks the strong tandem unless the strong tandem blitzes the B gap. Y will then block the defensive end by himself.

AST: Combo blocks the stack with Y. Attacks the defensive end and drives him backwards but keeps the strong tandem in his periphery. Continues to block the defensive end unless the strong tandem blitzes the B gap. If this situation occurs, AST will release pressure from the end and block the strong tandem.

ASG: Blocks Mike. If Mike blitzes weakside, ASG looks first for the weak tandem and then downfield.

C: Steps strong and blocks the nose.

BSG: Pulls and leads.

BST: Blocks the defensive end.

X: Blocks downfield.

QB: Reverse pivots but does not gain as much depth as he normally would on the power. After faking to the tailback, QB bootlegs and immediately locates Stud. If Stud is checking QB or pursuing the power, QB will toss a soft shovel pass to the slotback. If Stud is closing the off-tackle hole, QB will keep the ball. When in doubt, QB will pitch the ball into the dirt toward the line of scrimmage.

TB: Fakes the off-tackle power.

FB: Blocks Whip.

SB: Gains slight depth as he runs parallel to the line of scrimmage and prepares to receive a shovel pass from the quarterback. If the ball is passed to him, it is imperative that the SB secures the ball with both hands as he runs through traffic.

Tailback Bounce

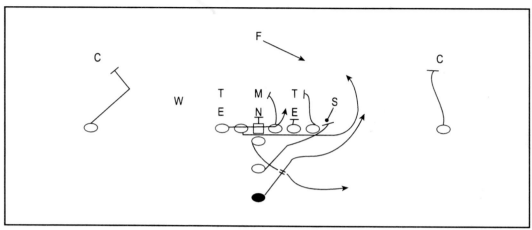

Diagram 4-8

Coaching Points: Because the tailback's first three steps are almost identical to the off-tackle power, this sweep variation freezes the inside sector of defense and drastically weakens its perimeter run support. This play should be called because Stud is closing hard inside and closing the off-tackle hole.

Y: Combo blocks the stack with the AST. Seals the C gap and bumps the defensive end. Works to the second level and blocks the strong tandem unless the strong tandem blitzes the B gap. Y will then block the defensive end by himself.

AST: Combo blocks the stack with Y. Attacks the defensive end and drives him backwards but keeps the strong tandem in his periphery. Continues to block the defensive end unless the strong tandem blitzes the B gap. If this situation occurs, AST will release pressure from the end and block the strong tandem.

ASG: Blocks Mike. If Mike blitzes weakside, ASG blocks the weak tandem.

C: Steps strong and blocks the nose.

BSG: Pulls and leads.

BST: Fills and leads through the attackside B gap if he encounters no backside penetration.

X: Blocks downfield.

QB: Reverse pivots and deals the ball to the tailback as deep as possible, and then fakes the quarterback keep.

TB: His first step is a cross-over step with his left foot. His next step is with his right foot and then his left. He will have possession of the ball by the time he makes his third step. He will then plant on his third step, break the play outside, and run to daylight.

FB: Blocks Stud. Attacks Stud's far hip and hooks him in.

Z: Blocks downfield.

Using Formations to Enhance the Tailback Bounce

Like the off-tackle power, a tight wing and tight slot formation can be used to augment the tailback bounce. Diagram 4-9A shows how the wingback can be used to seal Stud and thus enable the fullback and BSG to lead the tailback into the perimeter. The tight slot should only be used when Stud aligns inside of the tight end. When this situation occurs, the tight end will cave Stud inside and both the slotback and fullback will lead the tailback into the perimeter (Diagram 4-9B).

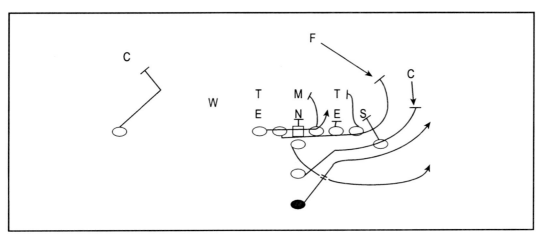

Diagram 4-9A

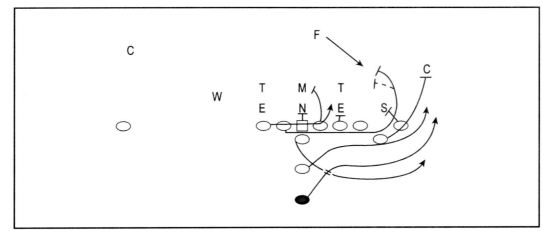

Diagram 4-9B

Bounce Option

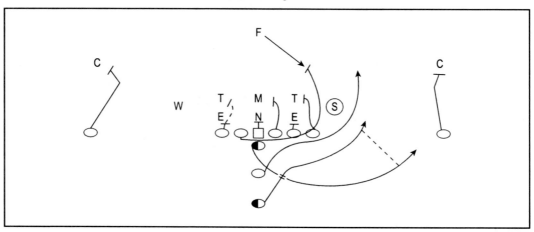

Diagram 4-10

Coaching Points: This play leaves Stud unblocked. Because Stud will be forced to tackle the tailback, the tailback will simply pitch the ball back to the quarterback as Stud approaches him. This play can also function as a shovel pass. When this is employed, the quarterback will fake the ball to the tailback. When Stud sees that the quarterback has the ball and attempts to tackle him, the quarterback will execute a soft shovel pass to the tailback. Another possible variation is to run the bounce option, as shown in Diagram 4-10, and then have the quarterback throw a forward pass after the tailback pitches the ball back to him.

Y: Combo blocks the stack with the AST. Seals the C gap and bumps the defensive end. Works to the second level and blocks the strong tandem unless the strong tandem blitzes the B gap. Y will then block the defensive end by himself.

AST: Combo blocks the stack with Y. Attacks the defensive end and drives him backwards but keeps the strong tandem in his periphery. Continues to block the defensive end unless the strong tandem blitzes the B gap. If this situation occurs, AST will release pressure from the end and block the strong tandem.

ASG: Blocks Mike. If Mike blitzes weakside, ASG blocks the weak tandem.

C: Steps strong and blocks the nose.

BSG: Pulls and blocks the free safety.

BST: Blocks the defensive end unless the defender slants outside. If this situation occurs, BST will work to the second level and block the weak tandem.

X: Blocks downfield.

QB: Reverse pivot and deal the ball to the tailback as deep as possible, and then trails behind the tailback in a good pitch position.

TB: Steps as he would on the bounce. Receives the ball from the quarterback and immediately locates Stud. As Stud attacks him, TB will execute a soft pitch to the quarterback.

FB: Leads downfield.

Z: Blocks downfield.

Quarterback Keep

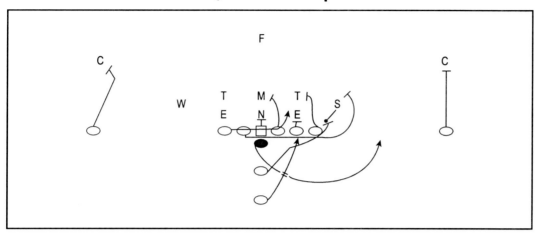

Diagram 4-11

Coaching Points: This play is a great complement for the off-tackle power when quarterback has decent potential to run the ball. It should be called when the secondary defender responsible for outside run support ignores the quarterback's fake or is playing soft. Like the tailback bounce, this play can be enhanced by using both a tight slot and tight wingback formation (use the same blocking assignments illustrated in Diagram 4-7).

Y: Combo blocks the stack with the AST. Seals the C gap and bumps the defensive end. Works to the second level and blocks the strong tandem unless the strong tandem blitzes the B gap. Y will then block the defensive end by himself.

AST: Combo blocks the stack with Y. Attacks the defensive end and drives him backwards but keeps the strong tandem in his periphery. Continues to block the defensive end unless the strong tandem blitzes the B gap. If this situation occurs, AST will release pressure from the end and block the strong tandem.

ASG: Blocks Mike. If Mike blitzes weakside, ASG blocks the weak tandem.

C: Steps strong side and blocks the nose.

BSG: Pulls and leads.

BST: Fills and leads through the attackside B gap if he encounterss no backside penetration.

X: Blocks downfield.

QB: Reverse pivots and makes a great fake to the tailback. Flashes the ball at the tailback with both hands and then quickly hides it on his right hip with his right hand as he simultaneously rides the tailback with his left hand. Hides the ball on his hip for as long as possible. Looking at the tailback after he fakes to him will enhance the effectiveness of the quarterback's fake.

TB: Fakes the off-tackle power. Makes a great fake by slapping his left elbow with his right hand and then running toward the off-tackle hole with great intensity.

FB: Blocks Stud. Attacks Stud's far hip and hooks him in.

Z: Blocks downfield.

Reverse

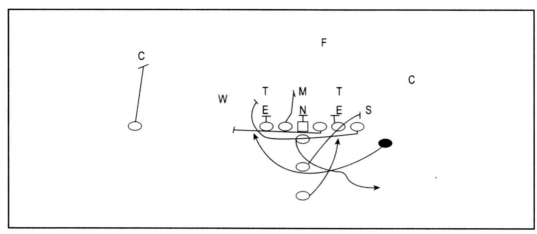

Diagram 4-12

Coaching Points: This play has a high potential for a fumble. As a result, the quarterback and wingback's execution must be meticulous.

Y: Pulls and leads.

AST: Blocks the defensive end.

ASG: Combo blocks the stack with the center. Seals the A gap and bumps the nose. Works to the second level and blocks Mike unless Mike blitzes the backside A gap. If this situation occurs, ASG will then block the nose by himself.

C: Combo blocks the stack with the ASG. Attacks the nose and drives him backwards but keeps Mike in his periphery. Continues to block the nose unless the Mike blitzes the backside A gap. If this situation occurs, the center will release pressure from the nose and block Mike.

BSG: Pulls and traps the first defender outside of the ASG's block.

BST: Blocks the defensive end. An exception would be if the end slants away from the play and the strong tandem blitzes into the B gap, then BST will release pressure on the end and block the strong tandem.

X: Blocks downfield.

QB: Reverse pivots and quickly seats the ball (i.e., brings the ball to his belt buckle). His reverse pivot will be as deep as the off-tackle power. Looks the ball into the wingback's pouch as he hands off. Does not fake to the tailback after the handoff. Instead, QB drops back as though he intends to pass.

TB: Fakes the off-tackle power.

FB: Blocks the first defender outside of the BST's block.

WB: Gains depth on his first step. Makes a good pouch. Secures the ball and protects it while in traffic. Runs to daylight.

Slotback Trap

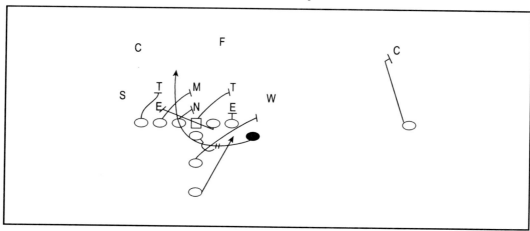

Diagram 4-13

Coaching Points: This play is very quick-hitting and also has a high potential for a fumble. Like the reverse, the quarterback and slotback's execution must be meticulous.

Y: Blocks the strong tandem. If the strong tandem blitzes into the B gap, Y will block downfield.

AST: Blocks Mike. If Mike blitzes, AST will block downfield.

ASG: Blocks the nose. If the nose slants away from the play, ASG will work to the second level and block Mike.

C: Blocks the weak tandem. If the nose slants into his path, Center will block the nose.

BSG: Pulls and traps the first defender outside of the ASG's block.

BST: Blocks the defensive end.

X: Blocks downfield.

QB: Steps back with his right foot as he seats the ball, reverse pivots, and quickly hands the ball to the slotback

TB: Fakes the off-tackle power.

FB: Blocks the first defender outside of the BST's block.

SB: Makes a good pouch. Secures the ball and protects it while in traffic. Runs to daylight.

Fullback Counter

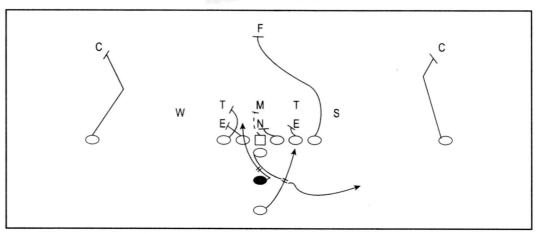

Diagram 4-14

Coaching Points: This play is another quick-hitting play that frequently catches the defense off guard.

Y: Blocks downfield.

AST: Folds inside and blocks the weak tandem. If the weak tandem blitzes into the C gap, AST will block downfield.

ASG: Blocks the defensive end.

C: Zones with the BSG. Steps strong and attacks the playside breastplate of the nose. Blocks the nose if he slants into the attackside A gap. Otherwise, the center will work to the second level and block Mike.

BSG: Zones with the center. Attacks the near breastplate of the nose. Blocks the nose unless he slants into the attackside A gap. If this situation occurs, BSG will work to the second level and blocks Mike.

BST: Blocks the end or the first defender that shows in the B gap.

X: Blocks downfield.

QB: Reverse pivots as he does on the power and gently hands the ball to the fullback.

TB: Fakes the off-tackle power. Makes a great fake by slapping his left elbow with his right hand and then running toward the off-tackle hole with great intensity.

FB: Jab steps with his right foot and momentarily pauses (it is imperative that the fullback is not in a big hurry). Takes his second step toward the hole with his left foot, makes a good pouch, secures the ball, and runs to daylight.

Z: Blocks downfield.

Counter Power

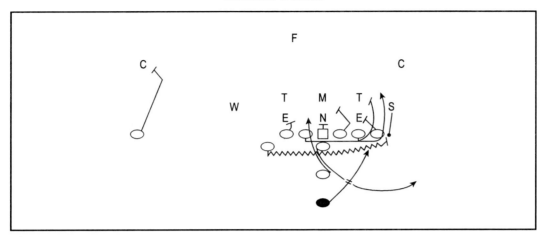

Diagram 4-15

Coaching Points: This variation of the power features excellent misdirection.

Y: Blocks the defensive end if the end plays straight or slants toward the C gap. If the end slants into the B gap, Y will work to the second level and block the strong tandem.

AST: Folds behind Y and blocks the strong tandem. If the strong tandem blitzes into the B gap, AST will block downfield.

ASG: Steps with right foot and blocks B gap penetration by either the strong end or tandem. If none, ASG will work to the second level and block Mike.

C: Drives the nose backwards at the snap. If the nose slants away from the play, the center will release pressure, work to the second level, and block Mike. Otherwise, the center will continue to drive the nose backwards.

BSG: Pulls and leads.

BST: Drives the end backwards at the snap. If the end slants away from the play, the BST will release pressure, work to the second level, and block the weak tandem. Otherwise, the BST will continue to drive the end backwards.

X: Blocks downfield.

QB: Reverse pivots and hands the ball as deep as possible to the tailback and then fakes the quarterback keep. The quarterback does not fake to the fullback.

TB: Steps directly at the hole. Does not look for the ball; it's the quarterback's responsibility to make the handoff. Protects the ball with both hands until he is out of traffic. Runs to daylight.

FB: Fakes the fullback counter and blocks any backside penetration.

SB: Goes into motion and blocks Stud.

Counter Trey

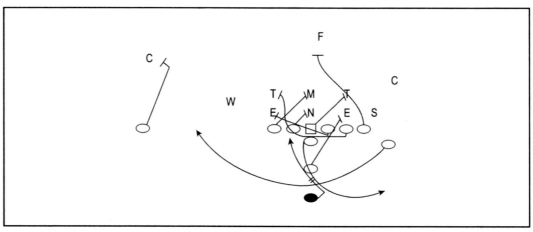

Diagram 4-16

Coaching Points: This play is an old play with a new twist added to it. By faking the wingback reverse, the defense is forced to defend both its inside sector and its perimeter, which slows defensive recognition and pursuit to the ball.

Y: Blocks the free safety.

AST: Blocks the Mike. If the end slants across his face, the AST will lock on to him and drive this defender inside.

ASG: Blocks the nose. If the nose slants away from the play, the ASG will work to the next level and block Mike.

C: Blocks the strong tandem. If the nose slants into his path, the center will block the nose.

BSG: Pulls and traps the first defender outside of the AST's block.

BST: Pulls and leads.

X: Blocks downfield.

QB: Reverses slightly deeper than he would for the off-tackle power. Deals the ball to the tailback, fakes to the wingback, and then pretends to run the naked boot.

TB: Makes his first step a cross-over step with his left foot. His next step will be with his right foot. He will plant on this step, cut toward the point of attack, receive the ball, and run to daylight.

FB: Blocks the first defender to pursue into the B gap.

WB: Fakes the reverse by making a good pouch and slapping his right elbow with his left hand as he passes the quarterback.

Trey Reverse

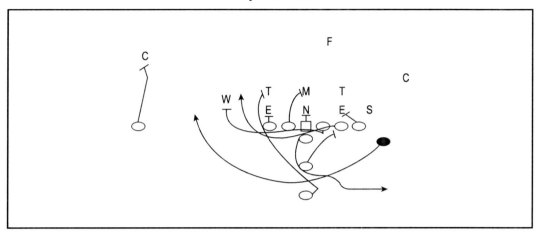

Diagram 4-17

Coaching Points: This play is the sequential counterpart of the counter trey that attacks the weakside perimeter.

Y: Blocks the defensive end or C gap penetration.

AST: Blocks the defensive end but keeps the weak tandem in his periphery. If the defensive end slants into the C gap and the weak tandem blitzes the B gap, AST will release pressure on the end and block the weak tandem

ASG: Blocks Mike.

C: Blocks the nose.

BSG: Pulls and blocks Whip.

BST: Pulls and leads.

X: Blocks downfield.

QB: Reverses pivots and conceals the ball from the defense by seating it until he hands of to the wingback. He then pretends to run the naked boot. It is not necessary for the quarterback to fake the ball to the tailback.

TB: Fakes the counter trey by slapping his right elbow with his left hand as he is passing the quarterback. TB will then block the first defender outside of the AST's block (usually this will be the weak tandem).

FB: Blocks the first defender to pursue into the B gap.

WB: Gains depth on his first step, receives the ball from the quarterback, and runs to daylight.

Naked Boot

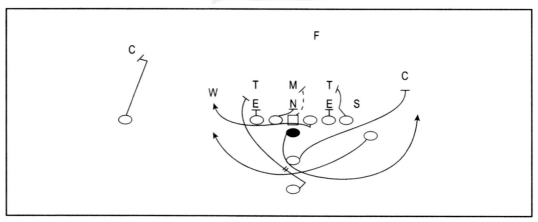

Diagram 4-18

Coaching Points: The quarterback should know when this play will be effective because he has been eyeballing Stud after his hand-offs on both the counter trey and trey reverse.

Y: Combo blocks the stack with the AST. Seals the C gap and bumps the defensive end. Works to the second level and blocks the strong tandem unless the strong tandem blitzes the B gap. Y will then block the defensive end by himself.

AST: Combo blocks the stack with Y. Attacks the defensive end and drives him backwards but keeps the strong tandem in his periphery. Continues to block the defensive end unless the strong tandem blitzes the B gap. If this situation occurs, AST will release pressure from the end and block the strong tandem.

ASG: Pulls opposite the play and blocks Whip.

C: Zones with the BSG. Steps strong and attacks the play side breastplate of the nose. Blocks the nose if he slants into the attackside A gap. Otherwise, the center will work to the second level and block Mike.

BSG: Zones with the center. Attacks the near breastplate of the nose. Blocks the nose unless the slants into the attackside A gap. If this situation occurs, BSG will work to the second level and block Mike.

BST: Blocks the defensive end but keeps the weak tandem in his periphery. If the defensive end slants into the C gap and the weak tandem blitzes the B gap, AST will release pressure on the end and block the weak tandem

X: Blocks downfield.

QB: Reverses pivots and conceals the ball from the defense by seating it until he fakes a hand-off to the wingback. He will then put the ball on his right hip and run the naked boot.

TB: Fakes the counter trey by slapping his right elbow with his left hand as he is passing the quarterback. TB will then block the first defender outside of the AST's block (usually this will be the weak tandem).

FB: Blocks the cornerback.

WB: Fakes the trey reverse.

Slotback Power

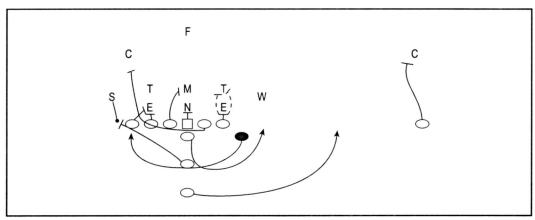

Diagram 4-19

Coaching Points: This variation of the power not only gives the slotback the opportunity to carry the ball but also sets up the power option.

Y: Double-teams the defensive end with the AST unless the end slants into the B gap (Y will then work to the second level and block the strong tandem) or the strong tandem blitzes the B gap, in which case Y will then block the defensive end by himself.

AST: Double-teams the defensive end with Y unless the defensive end slants into the B gap (AST will then block the end by himself) or the strong tandem blitzes the B gap, in which case AST will then release pressure from the defensive end and block the strong tandem.

ASG: Blocks Mike. If Mike blitzes weakside, ASG looks first for the weak tandem and then downfield.

C: Steps strong side and blocks the nose.

BSG: Pulls and leads.

BST: Attacks the end at the snap but sees the weak tandem out of his periphery. The moment BST sees the weak tandem's reaction to the play, he will release pressure on the end and block the weak tandem.

X: Blocks downfield.

QB: Pushes off his left foot, steps with his right foot, and opens up toward the slotback. After handing off the ball, the QB will run a flat course toward Whip.

TB: Fakes the power option away from the point of attack.

FB: Steps with his left foot directly toward the outside foot of the ASG, which enables the FB to gain an ideal kick out position on Stud. Blocks Stud at the hip and drives him outside.

SB: Goes into quick motion and begins to follow a path toward the near hip of the fullback and parallel to the line of scrimmage. Receives the ball from the quarterback and continues running parallel to the line of scrimmage until he is perpendicular to the hole. At this point, the slotback will make a right angle cut toward the hole.

Slotback Power Option

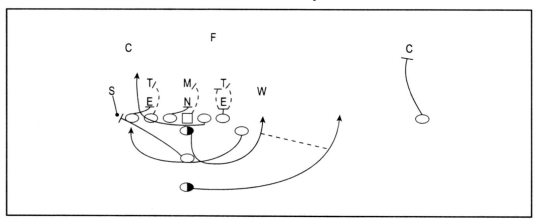

Diagram 4-20

Coaching Points: This play requires the defense to play forced assignment football versus the slotback power. If Whip is the only player assigned to both the tailback and quarterback, this play will be great. On the other hand, if two defenders are assigned to the option, the slotback power is enhanced because the defense is limited in its ability to pursue backside and play cutback.

Y: Zones the stack with the BST. Attacks the near breastplate of the defensive end and blocks the end unless he slants into the B gap. If this situation occurs, Y works to the next level and blocks the strong tandem

AST: Attacks the end at the snap but sees the weak tandem out of his periphery. The moment BST sees the weak tandem's reaction to the play, he will release pressure on the end and block the weak tandem.

ASG: Pulls opposite the point of attack.

C: Zones the stack with the BSG. Attacks the playside breastplate of the nose and blocks the nose if he slants into the attackside A gap. Otherwise, the center works to the second level and blocks Mike.

BSG: Zones the stack with the center. Attacks the near breastplate of the nose and blocks the nose unless he slants into the attackside A gap. If this situation occurs, BSG works to the next level and blocks Mike.

BST: Zones the stack with the Y. Attacks the playside breastplate of the defensive end and blocks the end if he slants into the B gap. Otherwise, BST works to the second level and blocks the strong tandem

X: Blocks downfield.

QB: Fakes the hand off to the slotback and options Whip. QB should be aggressive and run directly at Whip's inside shoulder forcing Whip to make an immediate decision.

TB: Runs an option course, maintaining a proper pitch relationship with the quarterback.

FB: Blocks Stud.

SB: Goes into quick motion and fakes the slotback power.

Augmenting the Power Series
with Play-Action Passes

Play-action passes are easily installed into the power series. Because specific pattern combinations will be discussed later in the book, this topic will not be covered in this section. The purpose of this section is to cover the overall structures into which the various pattern combinations can be integrated.

The first structure (Diagram 4-21A) is the best structure in football from which to launch a play-action pass. It is illustrated from a twins formation because this formation will (in most cases) reduce the 3-3-5 to a seven-man front and thus simplify pass protection. When this structure is employed, X, Z, and the fullback will run pass patterns. Because all three of the receivers are running their patterns toward the same side of the formation, this structure favors both flood and rub patterns. The tight end will block Stud if he rushes and run a designated outlet pattern if Stud drops into coverage. The tailback will fake the off-tackle power and make certain that the weak tandem does not tackle the quarterback. The best way for the tailback to accomplish this is to make a great fake and to get tackled. The interior linemen's responsibilities are as follows:

- **AST:** Block the weak end
- **ASG:** Block Mike
- **C:** Block the nose
- **BSG:** Block the strong tandem
- **BST:** Block the strong end

Diagram 4-21B the most appropriate structure to use when Whip remains in the box and the defense gives the offense a pre-snap look that indicates that it intends to employ zero coverage and send the house. The assignments for this structure are

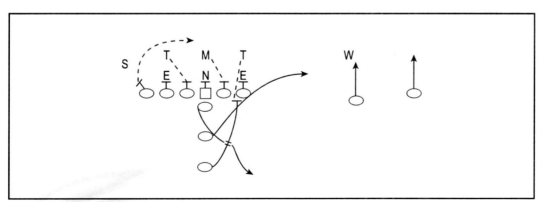

Diagram 4-21A

identical to the previous one with one exception. The fullback is now assigned to block Whip if he rushes and to run a designated outlet pattern if Whip drops into coverage.

Diagram 4-21C is similar to the first structure in that three receivers are being released on the same side of the formation. Rather than faking the off-tackle power, however, this structure features a counter trey fake. The assignments for this structure are identical to the first structure with two exceptions. The BSG is assigned to pull and block the weak tandem, and the tailback is responsible for blocking the strong tandem after he makes his fake.

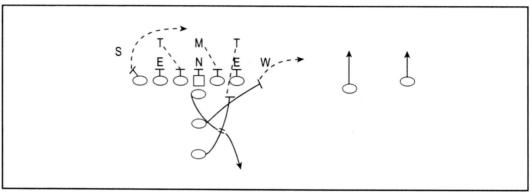

Diagram 4-21B

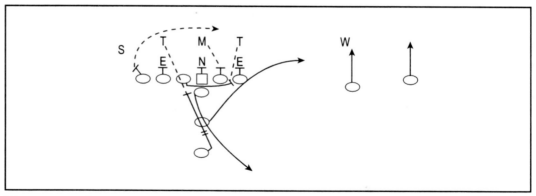

Diagram 4-21C

Play-action screens are also easily adaptable and extremely effective when installed into the power series. Diagram 4-22A illustrates a double screen that is initiated from a counter trey fake. The initial blocking assignments for interior linemen are identical to those of Diagram 4-21A. After executing these assignments for three seconds, the interior linemen will release to their illustrated screen assignments. Both the tight end and Z will block the two tandems if these defenders drop into coverage. If the tandems blitz, they will be blocked by the BSG and fullback long enough for the quarterback to throw the ball. The fullback is responsible for blocking the weak tandem if he blitzes and then for releasing to his pattern. The tailback should make a great fake and then release to his pattern. It should be noted that one of the major downfalls of failed screen plays is that the quarterback gets sacked because a player is in too big of a hurry to release to his screen responsibility and thus fails to execute his initial pass protection responsibility.

Diagram 4-22B illustrates another double screen that is initiated by an off-tackle fake. The primary receivers for this screen are the tight end and the tailback. The fullback will release into the flats and occupy Whip, and Z will block the weak tandem. The interior linemen's responsibilities are identical to the previous screen with one exception. The center will pull now pull strongside.

Diagram 4-22C illustrates a great screen that is initiated by a power reverse fake. When this screen is employed, the fullback will block stud and the tailback is responsible for blocking the strong tandem. X will block the weak tandem, and the interior linemen will employ the same rules that they used for the previous screen.

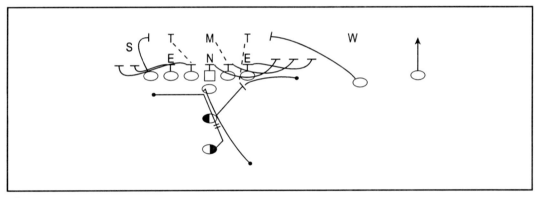

Diagram 4-22A

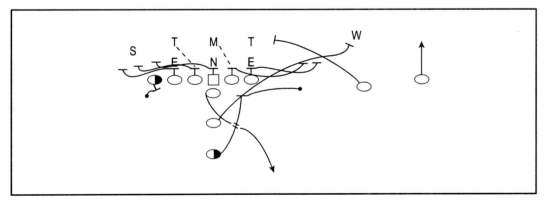

Diagram 4-22B

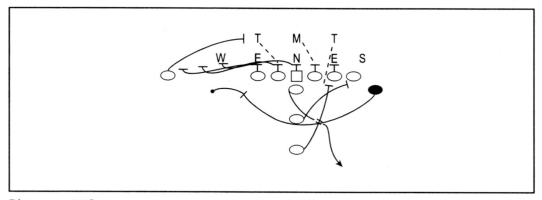

Diagram 4-22C

5

Attacking the 3-3-5 with the Gut Series

The gut series is the I formation's version of the wing-T. This quick-hitting series is initiated by first having the fullback attack the A gaps and then having the tailback attack either the off-tackle hole or perimeter. Because many defenses key the I formation fullback to determine the point of attack, this series denies the defense this key, reduces defensive play recognition, and inhibits pursuit and defensive aggressiveness. The gut series is a fully developed sequential series that features an abundance of misdirection and double binds.

Fullback Trap

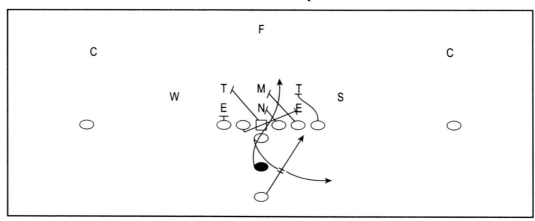

Diagram 5-1

Coaching Points: This quick-hitting trap play is the lead off play of the series.

Y: Blocks the strong tandem. If the strong tandem blitzes into the B gap, Y will block downfield.

AST: Blocks Mike. If Mike blitzes into the backside A gap, AST will block downfield.

ASG: Blocks the nose. If the nose slants away from the play, ASG will work to the second level and block Mike.

C: Blocks the strong tandem. If the nose slants or Mike blitzes into his path, the center will stop and block either defender.

BSG: Pulls and traps the first defender outside of the ASG's block.

BST: Blocks the defensive end.

X: Blocks downfield.

QB: Steps back with his right foot as he seats the ball, opens at 6 o'clock with his left foot, and quickly hands the ball to the fullback. Fakes the scissors.

TB: Fakes the tailback scissors.

FB: Cross-over steps with his right foot. Receives the ball as he makes his second step with his left foot. Cuts toward the hole on his second and reads the guard's block.

Z: Blocks downfield.

Tailback Scissors

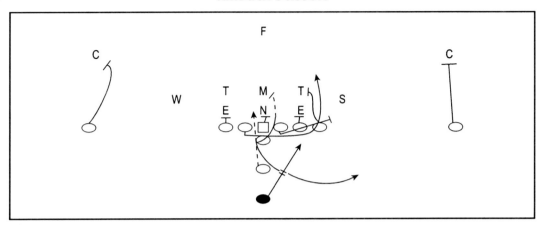

Diagram 5-2

Coaching Points: This quick hitting off-tackle play is one of the bread-and-butter plays of the series. The action of the fullback should freeze Mike long enough to prevent his pursuit to the point of attack.

Y: Combo blocks the stack with the AST. Seals the C gap and bumps the defensive end. Works to the second level and blocks the strong tandem unless the strong tandem blitzes the B gap. Y will then block the defensive end by himself.

AST: Combo blocks the stack with Y. Attacks the defensive end and drives him backwards but keeps the strong tandem in his periphery. Continues to block the defensive end unless the strong tandem blitzes the B gap. If this situation occurs, AST will release pressure from the end and block the strong tandem.

ASG: Pulls and traps Stud.

C: Drives the nose backwards at the snap but sees Mike out of his periphery. Player will continue to block the nose unless Mike blitzes through the attackside A gap. If this situation occurs, C will release pressure on the nose and block Mike.

BSG: Pulls and leads.

BST: Drives the defensive end backwards at the snap. If the defensive end slants away from the point of attack, BST will release pressure on the defensive end and block the weak tandem.

X: Blocks downfield.

QB: Reverse pivots as he seats the ball. Does not fake to the fullback. It is the fullback's responsibility to sell the fake. Hands the ball to the tailback and fakes a quarterback keep.

TB: Steps directly at the hole. Does not look for the ball; it's the quarterback's responsibility to make the handoff. Protects the ball with both hands until he is out of traffic. Runs to daylight.

FB: Cross-over steps with his right foot. Fakes the fullback trap as he makes his second step with his left foot by slapping his right elbow with his left hand. Continues on a course toward the backside A gap and blocks the nose if this defender slants into the backside A gap. If this does not occur, fullback will cut on his second step toward the attackside A gap and block Mike.

Z: Blocks downfield.

Scissors Trap

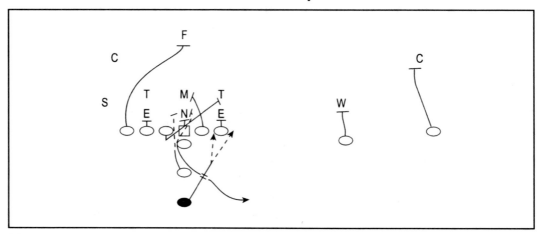

Diagram 5-3

Coaching Points: This variation of the scissors attacks the B gap and exploits a defense that frequently stunts.

Y: Blocks downfield.

AST: Drives the defensive end backwards at the snap and continues to block him unless the end slants inside. If this situation occurs, AST will release pressure on the end and block the weak tandem.

ASG: Blocks Mike

C: Blocks the nose

BSG: Pulls and traps the first defender to show in the B gap.

BST: Drives the defensive end backwards at the snap. If the defensive end slants away from the point of attack, BST will release pressure on the defensive end and block the weak tandem.

X: Blocks downfield.

QB: Reverse pivots as he seats the ball. Does not fake to the fullback. It is the fullback's responsibility to sell the fake. Hands the ball to the tailback and fakes a quarterback keep.

TB: Steps directly at the hole. Does not look for the ball; it's the quarterback's responsibility to make the handoff. Protects the ball with both hands as he reads the BSG's block.

FB: Cross-over steps with his right foot. Fakes the fullback trap as he makes his second step with his left foot by slapping his right elbow with his left hand. Continues on a course toward the backside A gap and blocks the nose if this defender slants into the backside A gap. If this does not occur, fullback will cut on his second step toward the attackside A gap and block Mike.

Z: Blocks downfield.

Gut Sweep

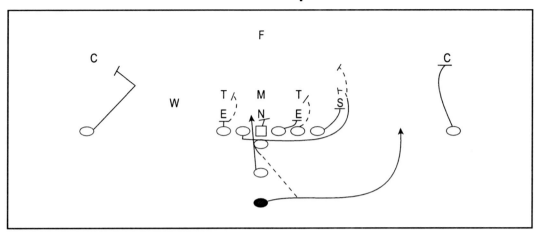

Diagram 5-4

Coaching Points: This sweep variation possesses the inherent advantage of momentarily freezing the linebackers and preventing their quick pursuit to the ball.

Y: Blocks Stud

AST: Zones the defensive end and strong tandem with the ASG. Steps with his outside foot and attacks the outside breastplate of the defensive end. AST will block the defensive end if he slants toward the C gap. Otherwise, he will work to the second level and block the strong tandem.

ASG: Zones the defensive end and strong tandem with the AST. Steps with his outside foot and attacks the inside breastplate of the defensive end. ASG will block the defensive end unless he slants toward the C gap. If this situation occurs, he will work to the second level and block the strong tandem.

C: Drives the nose backwards at the snap but sees Mike out of his periphery. Player will continue to block the nose unless Mike blitzes through the attackside A gap. If this situation occurs, C will release pressure on the nose and block Mike.

BSG: Pulls and leads.

BST: Drives the defensive end backwards at the snap. If the defensive end slants away from the point of attack, BST will release pressure on the defensive end and block the weak tandem.

X: Blocks downfield.

QB: Reverse pivots and pitches the ball to the tailback

TB: Runs parallel to the line, catches the ball, secures it and reads Y's block.

FB: Cross-over steps with his right foot. Quickly fakes the fullback trap as he makes his second step with his left foot (doesn't have time to make a good fake). Continues on a course toward the backside A gap and blocks the nose if this defender slants into the backside A gap. If this does not occur, fullback will cut on his second step toward the attackside A gap and block Mike.

Z: Blocks downfield.

Gut Sweep Variations

Diagrams 5-5A through 5-5C illustrate three variations of the gut sweep. Diagram 5-5A shows a weakside variation that employs a twins formation. This variation has the center and backside guard zoning Mike and the nose, and the attackside guard pulling and blocking the weak tandem. This option is an excellent choice when Whip shows a tendency to widen versus twins, but it is a bad choice versus zero coverage.

Diagram 5-5B shows a strongside variation that employs a wing formation. The blocking assignments for this variation are as follows:

- **Wing:** Blocks Stud

- **Y:** Blocks the defensive end unless the end slants inside. If this situation occurs, Y works to the second level and blocks the strong tandem.

- **AST:** Blocks Mike. If the end slant or the weak tandem blitzes across his face, AST stops and blocks either defender.

- **ACS:** Pulls and looks first for the strong tandem and second for the free safety.

- **BSG:** Pulls and leads.

- **BST:** Blocks the defensive end unless he slants away from the play. If this situation occurs, BST works to the second level and blocks the weak tandem.

The last variation is illustrated in Diagram 5-5C. This strongside variation is a good choice when Stud plays inside of the tight slot. The blocking assignments for this variation (except for Y and the slotback) are identical to those of Diagram 5-4.

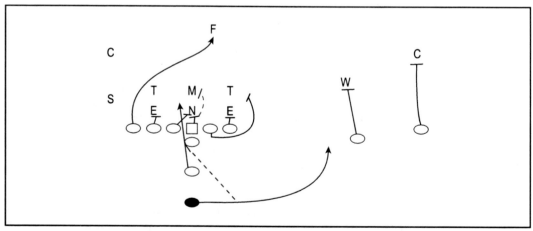

Diagram 5-5A

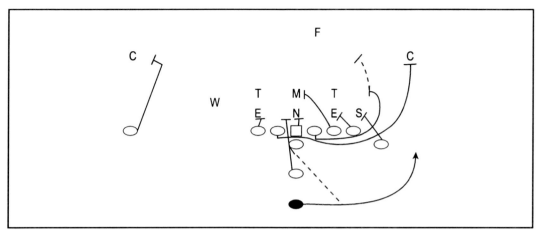

Diagram 5-5B

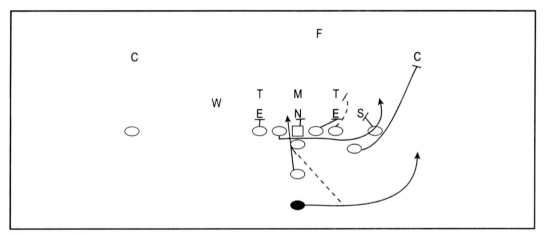

Diagram 5-5C

Gut Bounce

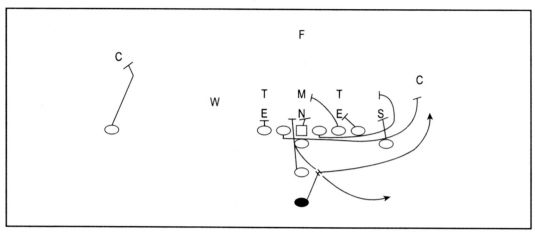

Diagram 5-6

Coaching Points: This play has all of the advantages of the tailback bounce plus the additional advantage of impairing defensive recognition and pursuit because of the action of the fullback.

Y: Blocks the defensive end unless the end slants inside. If this situation occurs, Y works to the next level and blocks the strong tandem.

AST: Blocks Mike unless the defensive end slants inside. If this situation occurs, AST blocks the end.

ASG: Pulls and looks first for the strong tandem. If this defender is blocked, ASG blocks the free safety.

C: Drives the nose backwards at the snap but sees Mike out of his periphery. Player will continue to block the nose unless Mike blitzes through the attackside A gap. If this situation occurs, C will release pressure on the nose and block Mike.

BSG: Pulls and leads.

BST: Drives the defensive end backwards at the snap. If the defensive end slants away from the point of attack, BST will release pressure on the end and block the weak tandem.

X: Blocks downfield.

QB: Reverse pivots as he seats the ball. Does not fake to the fullback. It is the fullback's responsibility to sell the fake. Hands the ball to the tailback and fakes a quarterback keep.

TB: His first step is a cross over step with his left foot. His next step is with his right foot and then his left. He will have possession of the ball by the time he makes his third step. He will plant on his third step, break the play outside, and then run to daylight.

FB: Cross-over steps with his right foot. Fake the fullback trap as he makes his second step with his left foot by slapping his right elbow with his left hand. Continues on a course toward the backside A gap and blocks the nose if this defender slants into the backside A gap. If this does not occur, fullback will cut on his second step toward the attackside A gap and block Mike.

WB: Blocks Stud.

Fullback Gut

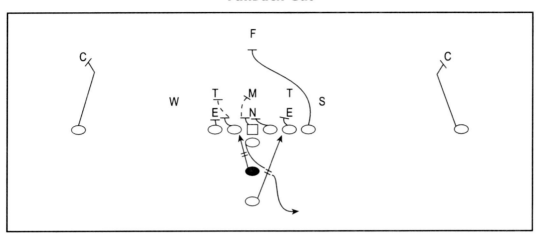

Diagram 5-7

Coaching Points: This weakside play is probably the quickest hitting play in football. It denies the defense easy play recognition when used in conjunction with the tailback gut.

Y: Blocks downfield.

AST: Zones with the ASG. Attacks the outside breastplate of the defensive end blocks this defender unless he slants inside. If this situation occurs, AST will block the weak tandem.

ASG: Zones with the AST. Attacks the inside breastplate of the defensive end blocks this defender if he slants inside. Otherwise ASG works to the second level and blocks the weak tandem.

C: Zones with the BSG. Steps weakside and attacks the playside breastplate of the nose. Blocks the nose if the nose slants into the attackside A gap. Otherwise, the center will work to the next level and block Mike.

BSG: Zones with the center. Attacks the near breastplate of the nose and blocks the nose unless the defender slants into the attackside A gap. If this situation occurs, BSG will block Mike

BST: Blocks the end or the first defender that shows in the B gap.

X: Blocks downfield.

QB: Steps back with his right foot as he seats the ball, opens at 6 o'clock with his left foot, and quickly hands the ball to the fullback

TB: Fakes the tailback scissors.

FB: Cross-over steps with his right foot. Receives the ball as he makes his second step with his left foot. Continues straight ahead or cuts backside on his second step as he reads the blocking scheme.

Z: Blocks downfield.

Tailback Gut

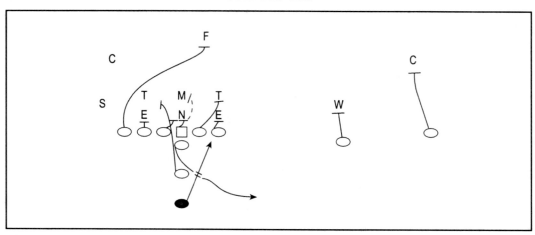

Diagram 5-8

Coaching Points: By running this play from twins, the offense is able to widen Whip and thus enable the tailback to break the play either inside or outside.

Y: Blocks downfield.

AST: Zones with the ASG. Attacks the outside breastplate of the defensive end blocks this defender unless he slants inside. If this situation occurs, AST will block the weak tandem.

ASG: Zones with the AST. Attacks the near breastplate of the defensive end blocks this defender if he slants inside. Otherwise ASG works to the second level and blocks the weak tandem.

C: Zones with the BSG. Steps playside and attacks the outside breastplate of the nose. Blocks the nose if the nose slants into the attackside A gap. Otherwise, the center will work to the next level and block Mike.

BSG: Zones with the center. Attacks the near breastplate of the nose and blocks the nose unless the defender slants into the attackside A gap. If this situation occurs, BSG will block Mike

BST: Blocks the end or the first defender that shows in the B gap.

X: Blocks downfield.

QB: Reverse pivots as he seats the ball. Does not fake to the fullback. Hands the ball to the tailback and fakes a quarterback keep.

TB: Steps directly at the hole. Receives the ball from the quarterback and protects it with both hands until he is out of traffic. Has the option of breaking the play inside or outside.

FB: Fakes the fullback gut. Makes a great fake.

Z: Blocks Whip.

Fullback Iso Gut

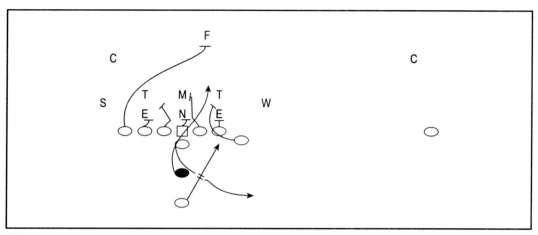

Diagram 5-9

Coaching Points: This play provides the offense with a different blocking scheme but the same backfield techniques as the fullback trap.

Y: Blocks downfield.

AST: Blocks the defensive end.

ASG: Steps inside, seals the A gap, and blocks Mike unless Mike stunts into the backside A gap. If this situation occurs, ASG double-teams the nose with the center.

C: Blocks the nose.

BSG: Step playside and blocks Mike if Mike stunts into the backside A gap. If this does not occur, BSG blocks the strong tandem.

BST: Blocks the defensive end unless the end slants away from the play. If this situation occurs, BST blocks the strong tandem.

X: Blocks downfield.

QB: Steps back with his right foot as he seats the ball, opens at 6 o'clock with his left foot, and quickly hands the ball to the fullback

TB: Fakes the tailback scissors.

FB: Cross-over steps with his right foot. Receives the ball as he makes his second step with his left foot. Cuts toward the hole on his second step and reads blocking pattern.

SB: Blocks the weak tandem.

Tailback Iso Gut

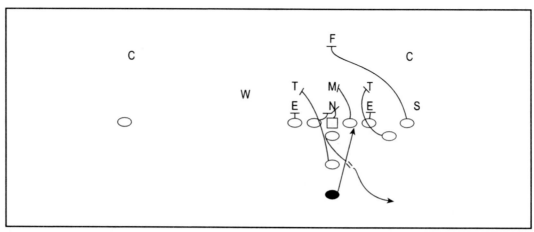

Diagram 5-10

Coaching Points: This play is excellent to use when Stud plays outside of the tight slot.

Y: Blocks downfield.

AST: Blocks the defensive end.

ASG: Blocks Mike

C: Double-teams the nose with the BSG. Attacks the nose's playside breastplate and drives him backwards.

BSG: Double-teams the nose with the center. Attacks the nose's near breastplate and drives him backwards.

BST: Blocks the defensive end unless the end slants away from the play. If this situation occurs, BST blocks the strong tandem.

X: Blocks downfield.

QB: Reverse pivots, hands the ball to the tailback as deep as possible, and fakes a quarterback keep.

TB: Steps directly at the hole, receives the ball from the quarterback, reads the blocking scheme, and runs to daylight.

FB: Fakes the fullback gut and blocks Mike if he stunts into the backside A gap. if this does not occur, TB blocks the weak tandem.

SB: Blocks the strong tandem.

Gut Reverse

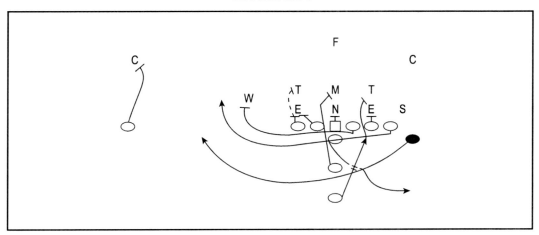

Diagram 5-11

Coaching Points: This great weakside play provides the offense with excellent misdirection.

Y: Pulls and leads.

AST: Zones the defensive end and weak tandem with the ASG. Attacks the outside breastplate of the end and blocks the end if he slants into the C gap. Otherwise, AST works to the second level and blocks the weak tandem.

ASG: Zones the defensive end and weak tandem with the AST. Attacks the near breastplate of the end and blocks the end unless he slants into the C gap. If this situation occurs, ASG works to the second level and blocks the weak tandem.

C: Blocks the nose

BSG: Pulls and blocks Whip.

BST: Blocks the defensive end. An exception is if the end slants away from the play and the strong tandem blitzes into the B gap, BST will release pressure on the end and block the strong tandem.

X: Blocks downfield.

QB: Reverse pivots, fakes to the tailback, hands the ball to the wingback, and fakes a quarterback keep.

TB: Fakes the scissors.

FB: Fakes the fullback gut and blocks Mike.

WB: Gains depth on his first step. Makes a good pouch. Secures the ball and protects it while in traffic. Runs to daylight.

Slotback Scissors

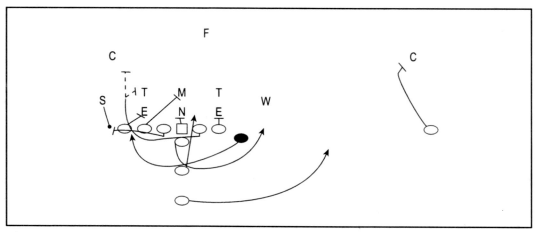

Diagram 5-12

Coaching Points: This play can be integrated into a series of its own that could include the fullback trap, the fullback gut, the slotback gut sweep, and the gut option.

Y: Blocks the defensive end unless this defender slants into the B gap. If this situation occurs, Y works to the next level and blocks the strong tandem.

AST: Blocks Mike unless the end slants into the B gap. If this situation occurs, AST will block the end.

ASG: Pulls and traps Stud.

C: Blocks the nose.

BSG: Pulls and leads.

BST: Drives the defensive end backwards at the snap. If the defensive end slants away from the point of attack, BST will release pressure on the defensive end and block the weak tandem.

X: Blocks downfield.

QB: Opens toward the slotback, hands the ball to the slotback, and fakes the gut option.

TB: Fakes the gut option.

FB: Fakes the gut and blocks Mike. If Mike is blocked, FB blocks the weak tandem.

SB: Gains depth on his first two steps, receives the ball from the quarterback, and runs to daylight.

Gut Option

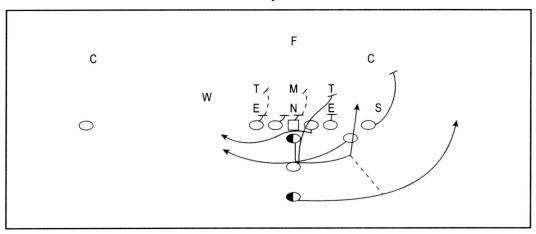

Diagram 5-13

Coaching Points: This play is an excellent call when Stud plays outside of the tight slot. It provides the offense with great misdirection and a false key.

Y: Arc releases and blocks the cornerback.

AST: Blocks the defensive end.

ASG: Pulls opposite the point of attack.

C: Zones the nose and Mike with the BSG. Attacks the playside breastplate of the nose and blocks the nose if he slants into the playside A gap. If this does not occur, the center works to the second level and blocks Mike.

BSG: Zones the nose and Mike with the center. Attacks the near breastplate of the nose and blocks the nose unless he slants into the playside A gap. If this situation occurs, BSG works to the second level and blocks Mike.

BST: Drives the defensive end backwards at the snap. If the defensive end slants away from the point of attack, BST will release pressure on the defensive end and block the weak tandem.

X: Blocks downfield.

QB: Opens toward the slotback, seats the ball, fakes a hand-off to the slotback, and options Stud.

TB: Establishes and maintains a good pitch relationship with the quarterback.

FB: Fakes the gut and blocks the weak tandem.

SB: Fakes the slotback scissors.

Augmenting the Gut Series with Play-Action Passes

Like the power series, play-action passes are easily installed into the gut series. Again, because specific pattern combinations will be discussed later in the book, this topic will not be covered in this section. The purpose of this section is to cover the overall structures that the various pattern combinations can be integrated into.

The first structure is illustrated in Diagram 5-14A. Like the majority of play-action passes presented in this book, it is illustrated from a twins formation because this formation will in most cases reduce the 3-3-5 to a seven-man front and thus simplify pass protection. The primary pass receivers in this first structure are X, Z, and the tailback. Both the tight end and fullback will run outlet routes if their assigned defender drops into coverage. The two guards will block the tandems, the tackles will block the ends, and the center will block the Nose.

The second structure is illustrated in Diagram 5-14B. The primary receivers are the fullback, X and Z. The tailback and tight end will run outlet patterns if their assigned defenders drop into coverage. The BSG and BST will zone the strong end and strong tandem. The center and ASG will zone Mike and the nose, and the AST will block the weak end.

The last structure is illustrated in Diagram 5-14C. The primary receivers are X, Y, and Z. The two running backs will run outlet routes. Both tackles will block the two defensive ends, and the BSG will pull and block Stud. The center and ASG will zone Mike and the nose, and the two running backs will check the two tandems before releasing into their outlet routes. Diagram 5-15 illustrates an excellent play-action screen that can easily be incorporated into the gut series.

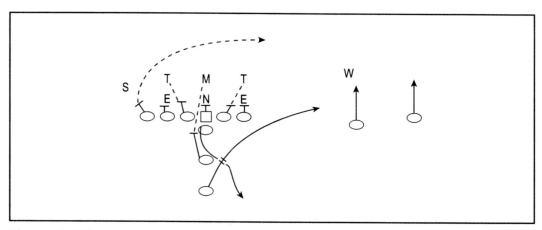

Diagram 5-14A

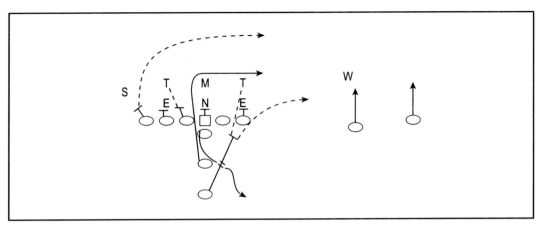

Diagram 5-14B

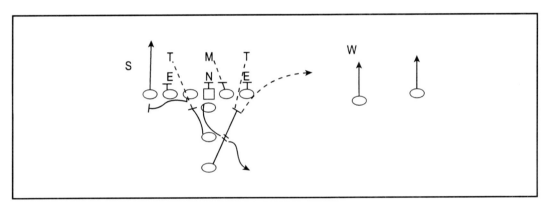

Diagram 5-14C

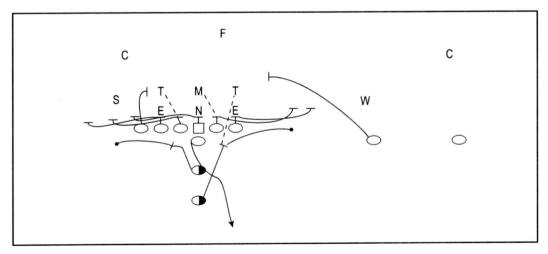

Diagram 5-15

6

Attacking the 3-3-5 with the Iso Series

The roots of this old series go back to Tom Nugent's I formation. This series attacks the inside sector of the defense, specifically the inside linebackers. Incorporated into the series are misdirection, option plays, play-action passes, and the strategic utilization of formations.

Tailback Iso

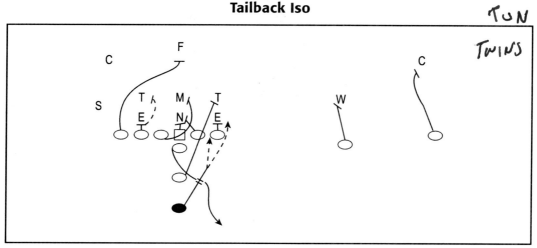

Diagram 6-1

Coaching Points: Tailback iso is the lead-off play of the series. By running it from a twins formation the offense is attempting to widen Whip and force the free safety to honor the quarterback keep, which will impair the safety's aggressiveness as an alley player.

Y: Blocks downfield.

AST: Blocks the defensive end.

ASG: Double-teams the nose with the center. Keeps Mike in his periphery. If Mike blitzes through the backside A gap, ASG will block the nose by himself.

C: Double-teams the nose with the ASG. Keeps Mike in his periphery. If Mike blitzes through the backside A gap, the center will release pressure on the nose and block Mike.

BSG: Pulls and blocks Mike. Some coaches may prefer to have the center and the ASG maintain their double-team on the nose no matter what happens and have the BSG eyeball Mike on his first step and block Mike if he blitzes the backside A gap.

BST: Drives the defensive end backward at the snap. If the defensive end slants away from the point of attack, BST will release pressure on the defensive end and block the strong tandem.

X: Blocks downfield.

QB: Gains depth by taking a short jab step straight backwards with his right foot as he seats the ball. Pivots on his first step and takes a long second step at 5 o'clock with his left foot. Hands the ball as deep as possible to the tailback and then either drops straight back and fakes a play-action pass or fakes a quarterback keep (depending upon each coaches preference).

TB: Steps directly at the hole. Does not look for the ball; it's the quarterback's responsibility to make the handoff. Protects the ball with both hands as he runs to daylight.

FB: Blocks the weak tandem.

Z: Blocks Whip.

Variations of the Tailback Iso

The blocking scheme presented in Diagram 6-1 is not the only scheme that can be used to run the iso against the 3-3-5. Diagrams 6-2A and 6-2B offer two additional schemes.

The assignments for interior linemen in the first variation (Diagram 6-2A) are as follows:

- **AST:** Blocks the defensive end.
- **ASG:** Blocks Mike.
- **C:** Double-teams the nose with the BSG. Attacks the nose's outside breastplate and drives the defender backwards.
- **BSG:** Double-teams the nose with the center. Attacks the nose's near breastplate and drives the defender backwards.
- **BST:** Blocks the defensive end unless he slants into the C gap. If this situation occurs, BST works to the next level and blocks the strong tandem.

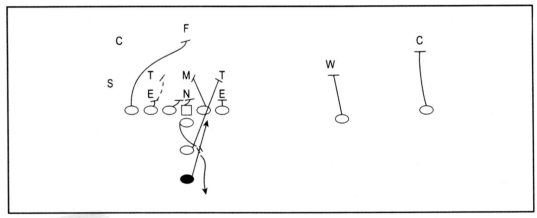

Diagram 6-2A

The assignments for interior linemen in the second variation (Diagram 6-2B) are as follows:

- **AST:** Blocks the defensive end.
- **ASG:** Double-teams the nose with the center unless Mike blitzes the backside A gap. If this situation occurs, ASG blocks the nose by himself.
- **C:** Double-teams the nose with the ASG unless Mike blitzes the backside A gap. If this situation occurs, the center will release pressure on the nose and block Mike.
- **BSG:** Blocks the strong tandem.
- **BST:** Blocks the defensive end.

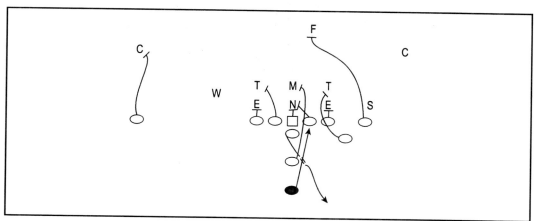

Diagram 6-2B

Iso Keep

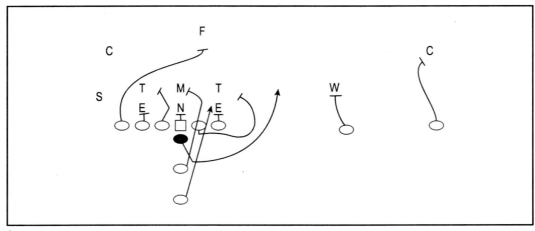

Diagram 6-3

Coaching Points: This play is good for a mobile quarterback. It is most effective when the eye in the sky has determined that the free safety is playing the alley 100 percent and neglecting to check the quarterback.

Y: Blocks downfield.

AST: Blocks the defensive end.

ASG: Pulls and blocks the weak tandem.

C: Blocks the nose.

BSG: Checks Mike for a blitz into the backside A gap. If this does not occur, BSG blocks the strong tandem.

BST: Drives the defensive end backward at the snap. If the defensive end slants away from the point of attack, BST will release pressure on the defensive end and block the strong tandem.

X: Blocks downfield.

QB: Gains depth by taking a short jab step straight backwards with his right foot as he seats the ball. Pivots on his first step and takes a long second step at 5 o'clock with his left foot. Fakes to the tailback, hides the ball on his right hip, and runs to daylight.

TB: Fakes the iso and then blocks the weak tandem if he blitzes into the B gap.

FB: Blocks Mike.

Z: Blocks Whip.

Iso Option

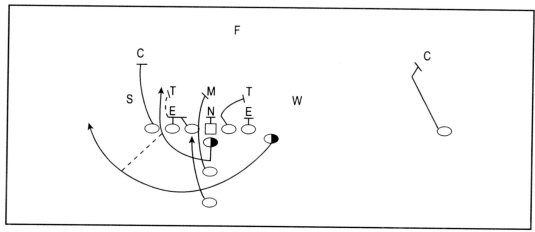

Diagram 6-4

Coaching Points: Woody Hayes used this play successfully when his Ohio State team won the 1968 Rose Bowl. It is still a great play!

Y: Blocks downfield.

AST: Zones the strong end and tandem with the ASG. Attacks the outside breastplate of the end and blocks the end if he slants into the C gap. Otherwise, AST will work to the second level and block the strong tandem.

ASG: Zones the strong end and tandem with the AST. Attacks the near breastplate of the end and blocks the end unless he slants into the C gap. If the end slants into the C gap, ASG will work to the next level and block the strong tandem.

C: Blocks the nose.

BSG: Checks Mike for a blitz into the backside A gap. If this does not occur, BSG blocks the strong tandem.

BST: Drives the defensive end backward at the snap. If the defensive end slants away from the point of attack, BST will release pressure on the defensive end and block the strong tandem.

X: Blocks downfield.

QB: Steps sideways with his right foot and then step back with his left foot so that his shoulders are perpendicular to the line of scrimmage. Fakes to the tailback and then options Stud. The quarterback must be aggressive and run directly at Stud. If he keeps the ball, he will plant on his downfield foot and immediately get his shoulders parallel to the line of scrimmage. If he pitches it, he will make a one-handed basketball pass from his heart to the tailback's heart.

TB: Fakes the iso. May have to cheat up slightly.

FB: Blocks Mike.

SB: Establishes and maintains a good pitch relationship with the quarterback. Some slotbacks may have to go into quick motion to accomplish this maneuver.

Iso Reverse

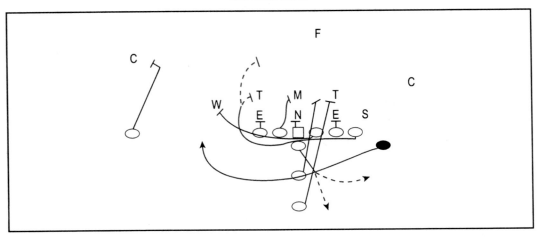

Diagram 6-5

Coaching Points: This play gives the series misdirection. Misdirection can also be added to the base play by faking this reverse and running the iso.

Y: Pulls and leads.

AST: Blocks the defensive end.

ASG: Combo blocks with the center. If the nose slants into the attackside A gap and Mike blitzes the backside A gap, ASG blocks the nose. If the nose plays straight (or slants into the backside A gap), ASG works to the second level and blocks Mike.

C: Combo blocks with the ASG. Drives the nose backwards at the snap and sees Mike out of his periphery. If the nose slants into the attackside A gap and Mike blitzes into the backside A gap, the center will release pressure on the nose and block Mike. Otherwise, the center will stay locked on the nose.

BSG: Pulls and traps the first defender outside of the AST's block.

BST: Blocks the defensive end. An exception is if the end slants away from the play and the strong tandem blitzes into the B gap, BST will release pressure on the end and block the strong tandem.

X: Blocks downfield.

QB: Fakes the tailback iso, hands the ball to the wingback, and either fakes a quarterback keep or play-action pass.

TB: Fakes the tailback iso and blocks the strong tandem.

FB: Blocks Mike.

WB: Gains depth on his first step. Makes a good pouch. Secures the ball and protects it while in traffic. Runs to daylight.

Fullback Iso

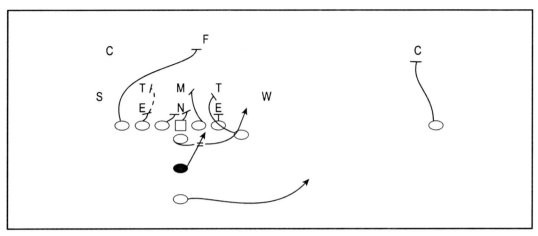

Diagram 6-6

Coaching Points: This quick-hitting iso renders itself to a number of excellent sequential complements. It also gives the I fullback additional opportunities to carry the ball.

Y: Blocks downfield.

AST: Blocks the defensive end.

ASG: Blocks Mike

C: Double-teams the nose with the BSG. Attacks the playside breastplate of the nose and drives him backwards.

BSG: Double-teams the nose with the center. Attacks the near breastplate of the nose but keeps Mike in his periphery. If Mike blitzes the backside A gap, BSG will release pressure on the nose and block Mike. Otherwise, BSG will continue his double-team with the center.

BST: Drives the defensive end backward at the snap. If the defensive end slants away from the point of attack, BST will release pressure on the defensive end and block the strong tandem.

X: Blocks downfield.

QB: Reverse pivots and quickly hands the ball off the fullback. Fakes the option keep.

TB: Fakes the option keep.

FB: Steps with his near foot directly at the outside foot of the ASG (some coaches may prefer the fullback's first step to be a cross-over step). Secures the ball with both hands as he bursts through the hole.

SB: Blocks the weak tandem.

Option Keep

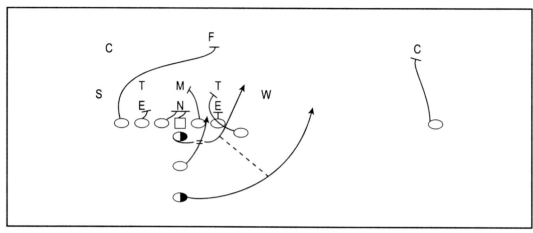

Diagram 6-7

Coaching Points: This play attacks the perimeter by faking the fullback iso.

Y: Blocks downfield.

AST: Blocks the defensive end.

ASG: Blocks Mike

C: Double-teams the nose with the BSG. Attacks the playside breastplate of the nose and drives him backwards.

BSG: Double-teams the nose with the center. Attacks the near breastplate of the nose but keeps Mike in his periphery. If Mike blitzes the backside A gap, BSG will release pressure on the nose and block Mike. Otherwise, BSG will continue his double-team with the center.

BST: Drives the defensive end backward at the snap. If the defensive end slants away from the point of attack, BST will release pressure on the defensive end and block the strong tandem.

X: Blocks downfield.

QB: Reverse pivots and fakes the fullback iso. Attempts to run uphill as he aggressively attacks the Whip's inside shoulder and forces the defender to make a quick decision.

TB: Establishes and maintains a good pitch relationship with the quarterback.

FB: Fakes the fullback iso.

SB: Blocks the weak tandem. The slotback is in an ideal position to read and react to the movements of the weak tandem. Normally, the slotback will go through the B gap to block this defender, but if the weak tandem blitzes through the C gap, the slotback will have ample time to redirect his course.

Slotback Counter

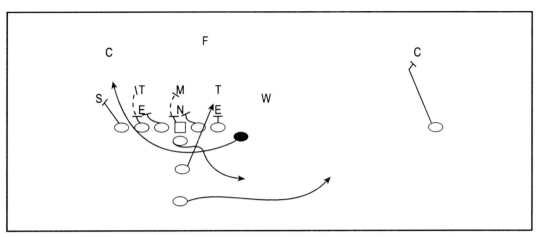

Diagram 6-8

Coaching Points: This play frequently results in a big gain when the strongside cornerback over reacts to the backfield flow.

Y: Blocks Stud.

AST: Zones with the ASG. Attacks the outside breastplate of the defensive end blocks this defender if he slants outside. Otherwise, AST will work to the second level and block the strong tandem.

ASG: Zones with the AST. Attacks the inside breastplate of the defensive end blocks this defender unless he slants outside. If the end slants outside, ASG works to the second level and blocks the strong tandem.

C: Zones with the BSG. Steps with his left foot and attacks the playside breastplate of the nose. Blocks the nose if the nose slants into the attackside A gap. Otherwise, the center will work to the next level and block Mike.

BSG: Zones with the center. Attacks the near breastplate of the nose and blocks the nose unless the defender slants into the attackside A gap. If this situation occurs, BSG will block Mike

BST: Blocks the defensive end.

X: Blocks downfield.

QB: Reverse pivots, fakes to the fullback, hands the ball to the slotback, and then either fakes a keep or a play-action pass.

TB: Fakes the option keep.

FB: Fakes the fullback iso and then looks to block the weak tandem if this defender blitzes through the B gap.

SB: Gains slight depth on his first step and immediately directs his course to the mesh point. Receives the ball from the quarterback and reads the blocks of Y and the AST. Has the option of breaking the play into the C or D gaps.

Fullback Counter Give

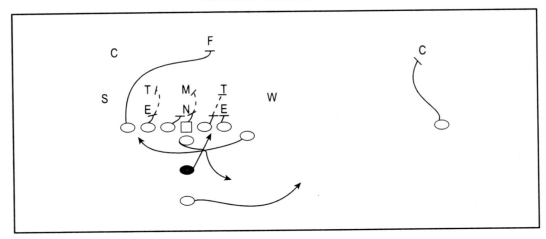

Diagram 6-9

Coaching Points: This play was instrumental in one of our state championship wins. As the defense comes to recognize the slotback counter, this play frequently results in very big gains.

Y: Blocks downfield.

AST: Zones with the ASG. Attacks the outside breastplate of the defensive end. Blocks this defender unless he slants inside. If this situation occurs, AST will block the weak tandem.

ASG: Zones with the AST. Attacks the inside breastplate of the defensive end blocks this defender if he slants inside. Otherwise, ASG works to the second level and blocks the weak tandem.

C: Zones with the BSG. Steps weakside and attacks the playside breastplate of the nose. Blocks the nose if the nose slants into the attackside A gap. Otherwise, the center will work to the next level and block Mike.

BSG: Zones with the center. Attacks the near breastplate of the nose and blocks the nose unless the defender slants into the attackside A gap. If this situation occurs, BSG will block Mike

BST: Blocks the defensive end unless the end slants into the C gap. If this situation occurs BST works to the next level and blocks the strong tandem

X: Blocks downfield.

QB: Reverse pivots, hands the ball to the fullback, fakes a handoff to the slotback, and then either fakes a keep or a play-action pass.

TB: Fakes the option keep.

FB: Steps with his near foot directly at the outside foot of the ASG. Secures the ball with both hands as he bursts through the hole.

SB: Fakes the slotback counter.

Enhancing the Iso Series with Play-Action Passes

Probably the best play-action to evolve from this series is fake iso boot (Diagram 6-10). When this is implemented, the three primary receivers are X, Y, and Z. The fullback is assigned an outlet route. The specific assignments for interior linemen are as follows:

- **AST:** Zones the weak tandem and weak end with the ASG. Blocks the tandem if he blitzes through the C gap. Otherwise, blocks the end.

- **ASG:** Zones the weak tandem and weak end with the AST. Blocks the tandem or end if either player slants or blitzes through the B gap. Otherwise, helps the AST block the end.

- **C:** Blocks the nose unless the nose slants into the backside A gap and Mike blitzes into the attackside A gap. If this situation occurs, the center blocks Mike.

- **BSG:** Pulls and blocks Whip.

- **BST:** Blocks the strong end.

An excellent screen that sequentially complements the slotback counter is illustrated in (Diagram 6-11). When this screen is used, the quarterback should see the Whip out of his periphery as he fakes to the fullback. If he sees Whip rushing from the edge, he should gain depth as the slotback clears his path and dump the ball off to the tailback. If the Whip does not rush, the quarterback will throw the screen to the slotback.

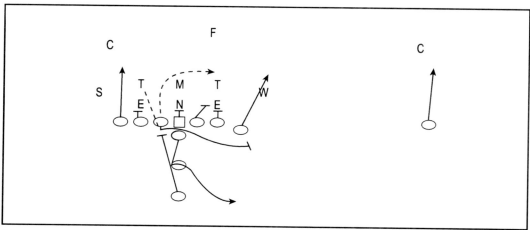

Diagram 6-10

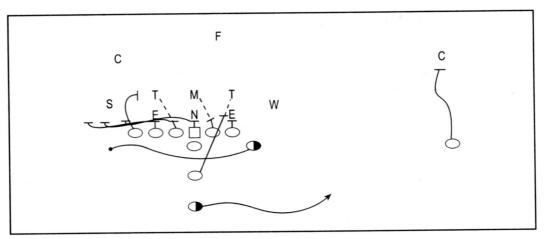

Diagram 6-11

7

Attacking the 3-3-5
with the Stampede Series

The lead-off play of this series attacks the perimeter of the defense and frequently results in huge gains. Its roots go back to the single wing. Both Vince Lombardi and John McKay made the stampede the staple of their offense. Although the stampede gives the defense a full flow key, the series is augmented with enough sequence and misdirection to hold the defense accountable for initially staying at home and checking counter and reverse before pursuing the toward the perimeter.

Tailback Stampede

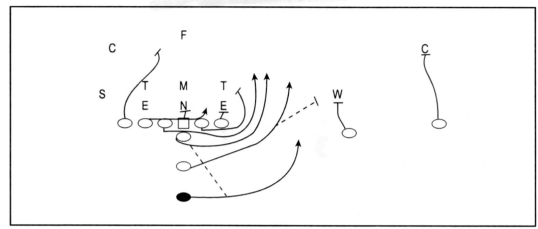

Diagram 7-1

Coaching Points: This play, often referred to as "student body right," was made famous by John McKay. Although it can be run from a pro formation, a twin formation often results in Whip widening. This approach relieves the offense from having to block an extra defender aligned in the box.

Y: Blocks downfield.

AST: Blocks the defensive end. Hooks the defender inside.

ASG: Pulls and blocks the weak tandem.

C: Blocks the nose.

BSG: Pulls and leads.

BST: Fills through the attackside B gap. Blocks any penetration that may get in his path.

X: Blocks downfield.

QB: Takes a short jab step parallel to the line of scrimmage with his right foot. Pivots on his right foot and simultaneously tosses the ball (dead ball toss) to the tailback and then leads the pack into the end zone.

TB: Steps parallel to the line with his right foot. Looks the ball into his hands as he receives the toss from the quarterback. Immediately secures the ball into his right hand and finds the end zone.

FB: Leads the play. First looks outside and then upfield.

Z: Blocks downfield.

Enhancing the Stampede with Wing and Slot Formations

When Stud plays inside of a tight slot, the tight end will crack block Stud and the slotback will block the cornerback (Diagram 7-2A). Everyone else's assignment remains identical to the previous version of the stampede.

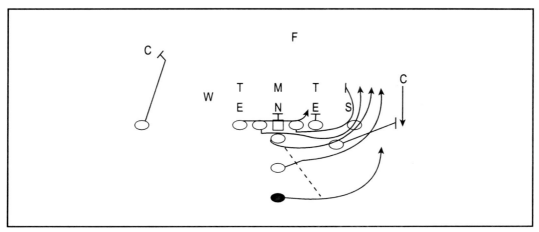

Diagram 7-2A

A tight wing formation (Diagram 7-2B) will usually force Stud into a 9 technique. When this situation occurs, the wingback will crack block Stud, Y will block the defensive end (or first show in the C gap), and the AST will block Mike (or first show in the B gap). Everyone else's assignment remains unchanged.

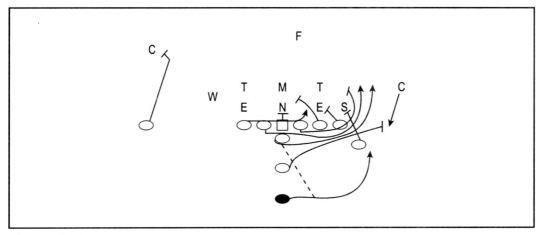

Diagram 7-2B

Power Toss

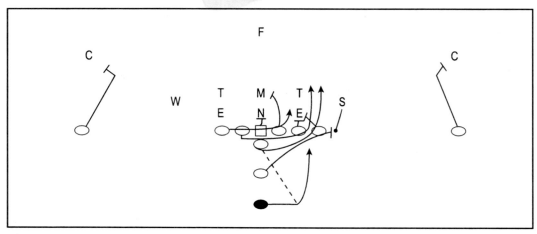

Diagram 7-3

Coaching Points: This off-tackle play double not only attains a double-team at the point of attack but also has two blockers leading the ballcarrier through the hole.

Y: Double-team the defensive end with the AST unless the end slants into the B gap (Y will then block the strong tandem), or the strong tandem blitzes the B gap, in which case Y will then block the defensive end by himself.

AST: Double-teams the defensive end with Y unless the defensive end slants into the B gap (AST will then block the end by himself), or the strong tandem blitzes the B gap, in which case AST will then release pressure from the defensive end and block the strong tandem.

ASG: Blocks Mike. If Mike blitzes weakside, ASG looks first for the weak tandem and then downfield.

C: Steps strongside and blocks the nose.

BSG: Pulls and leads.

BST: Fills and leads through the attackside B gap. Blocks any defensive penetration along the way.

X: Blocks downfield.

QB: Takes a short jab step parallel to the line of scrimmage with his right foot. Pivots on his right foot and simultaneously tosses the ball (dead ball toss) to the tailback and maintains a shoulder-to-shoulder relationship with the BSG as he leads the tailback through the hole.

TB: Steps first with his right foot and then takes two more steps parallel to the line. Looks the ball into his hands as he receives the toss from the quarterback and immediately secures the ball into his right hand. Plants on his third step (right foot) and follows his blockers through the hole.

FB: Steps with his right foot directly toward the outside foot of the ASG, enabling the FB to gain an ideal kick-out position on Stud. Blocks Stud at the hip and drives him outside.

Z: Blocks downfield.

Intensifying the Power Toss with a Wing and Slot

Like the stampede, the power toss can be enhanced by both wing and slot formations. The slot puts Stud in an alignment dilemma. As previously noted, if Stud plays inside of the slot he is vulnerable to the stampede. On the other hand, if he plays outside of the slot, he becomes vulnerable to the power toss (Diagram 7-4A).

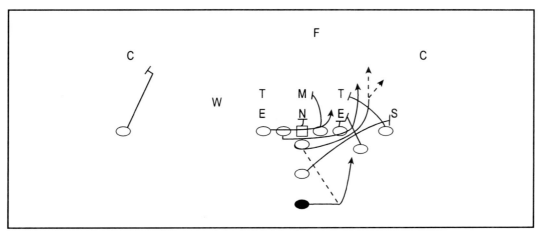

Diagram 7-4A

A tight wing formation can be used to double-bind Stud. By having the wingback pretending to crack on Stud before blocking the strong tandem, Stud is faced with the dilemma of either ignoring the wingback and becoming vulnerable to the stampede, or fighting outside and becoming vulnerable to the power toss (Diagram 7-4B).

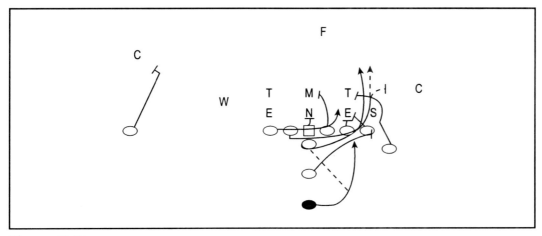

Diagram 7-4B

Toss Trey

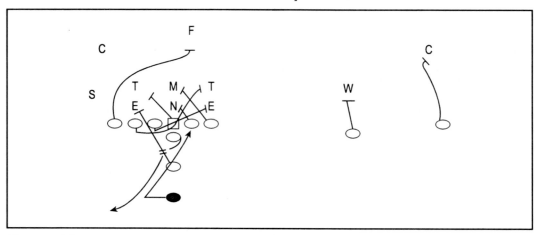

Diagram 7-5

Coaching Points: The purpose of running this play toward the two-receiver side of the formation is to reduce the number of players in the box. Although the power toss was illustrated from pro, wing, and slot formations, it can also be run from a twin formation (toward Y). This approach denies the defense a key that would help it predict the toss trey.

Y: Blocks the free safety.

AST: Blocks Mike. If the end slants across his face, the AST will lock on to him and drive this defender inside.

ASG: Blocks the nose. If the nose slants away from the play, the ASG will work to the next level and block Mike.

C: Blocks the strong tandem. If the nose slants into his path, the center will block the nose.

BSG: Pulls and traps the first defender outside of the AST's block.

BST: Pulls and leads.

X: Blocks downfield.

QB: Reverse pivots and fakes a toss to the tailback. It is important that the quarterback really emphasizes his fake toss. Quarterback will then gain depth, hand the ball to the tailback, and fake the bootleg.

TB: Takes three quick steps parallel to the line before cutting toward the hole. His first step is a slight jab step with his left foot, followed by two more steps. Tailback will fake catching the toss on these last two steps; he will then plant on his third step (left foot) and cut toward the hole. After receiving the ball from the quarterback, the tailback will secure the ball and run to daylight.

FB: Blocks the first defender to pursue into the B gap.

Z: Blocks Whip.

Slotback Trap

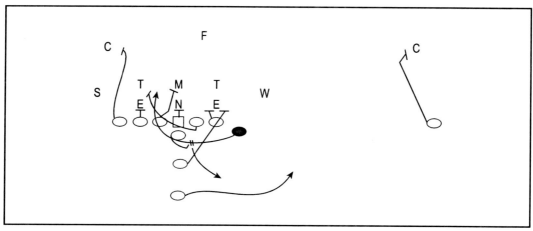

Diagram 7-6

Coaching Points: Unlike most of the traps that have been presented thus far, this play is a linebacker trap. If the trapped linebacker (strong tandem) were to stunt in the C gap, the pulling guard would trap the defensive end and his block would turn out to be a double-team with the AST.

Y: Blocks the cornerback.

AST: Blocks the defensive end.

ASG: Combo blocks the stack with the center. If the nose slants into the attackside A gap, ASG blocks him. If the nose plays straight, or slants into the backside A gap, ASG works to the second level and blocks Mike.

C: Combo blocks the stack with the ASG. Drives the nose backwards at the snap. If the nose slants into the attackside A gap and Mike blitzes into the backside A gap, the center will release pressure on the nose and block Mike. Otherwise, the center will stay locked on the nose.

BSG: Pulls and traps the strong tandem. If the strong tandem stunts himself out of the play, the BSG will trap the defensive end (double-team with the AST).

BST: Blocks the defensive end.

X: Blocks downfield.

QB: Gains depth by taking a quick jab step with his right foot (backwards at a 45-degree angle), reverse pivots, and quickly fakes a toss to the tailback. Quarterback then hands the ball to the slotback and bootlegs away from the point of attack.

TB: Fakes the stampede.

FB: Blocks the first defender outside of the BST's block.

SB: Gains slight depth on his first step, receives the hand-off, secures the ball, and follows the block of the pulling guard.

Fake Trey-Boot

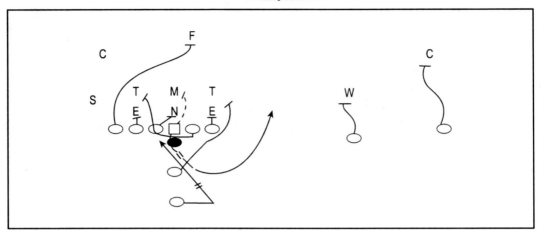

Diagram 7-7

Coaching Points: This bootleg, which attempts to confound the defense with a false key (the pulling guard), provides the offense with a valuable tool that enables it to utilize the talents of the swift-footed quarterback. By running it from a twins formation, the offense is able to reduce the number of defenders in the box to seven.

Y: Blocks downfield.

AST: Blocks the defensive end. Attacks the defenders outside breastplate and hooks him in.

ASG: Pulls and blocks the strong tandem.

C: Zones the stack with the BSG. Steps with his right foot and attacks the playside breastplate of the nose. Blocks the nose if the nose slants into the attackside A gap. Otherwise, the center will work to the next level and block Mike.

BSG: Zones the stack with the center. Attacks the near breastplate of the nose and blocks the nose unless the defender slants into the attackside A gap. If this situation occurs, BSG will block Mike.

BST: Blocks the defensive end.

X: Blocks downfield.

QB: Reverse pivots and fakes the toss trey. Hides the ball on his right hip and bootlegs into the perimeter.

TB: Fakes the toss trey and then blocks backside penetration.

FB: Blocks the weak tandem.

Z: Blocks Whip.

Fake Trap-Boot

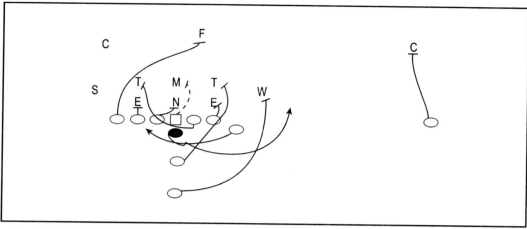

Diagram 7-8

Coaching Points: This bootleg provides the offense with the same advantages of the trey boot but employs different backfield action.

Y: Blocks downfield.

AST: Blocks the defensive end. Attacks the defenders outside breastplate and hooks him in.

ASG: Pulls and blocks the strong tandem.

C: Zones the stack with the BSG. Steps weakside and attacks the playside breastplate of the nose. Blocks the nose if the nose slants into the attackside A gap. Otherwise, the center will work to the next level and block Mike.

BSG: Zones the stack with the center. Attacks the near breastplate of the nose and blocks the nose unless the defender slants into the attackside A gap. If this situation occurs, BSG will block Mike.

BST: Blocks the defensive end.

X: Blocks downfield.

QB: Fakes the slotback trap. Hides the ball on his right hip and bootlegs into the perimeter.

TB: Fakes the tailback stampede and then blocks Whip.

FB: Blocks the weak tandem.

SB: Fakes the slotback trap.

Fake Stampede-Reverse

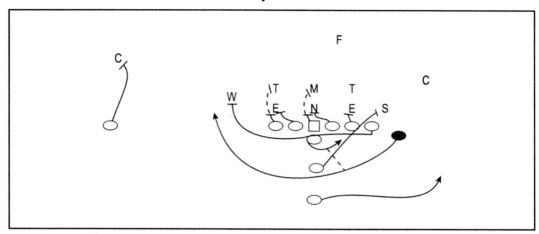

Diagram 7-9

Coaching Points: The fake stampede-reverse is a great misdirection play that exploits over-pursuing defenses.

Y: Pulls and leads. Blocks the first defender outside of the AST's block.

AST: Zones with the ASG. Attacks the outside breastplate of the defensive end. Blocks this defender if he slants outside. Otherwise, AST will work to the second level and block the weak tandem.

ASG: Zones with the AST. Attacks the inside breastplate of the defensive end. Blocks this defender if he slants outside. If this situation occurs, ASG works to the second level and blocks the weak tandem.

C: Zones with the BSG. Steps with his left foot and attacks the playside breastplate of the nose. Blocks the nose if the nose slants into the attackside A gap. Otherwise, the center will work to the next level and block Mike.

BSG: Zones with the center. Attacks the near breastplate of the nose and blocks the nose unless the defender slants into the attackside A gap. If this situation occurs, BSG will block Mike

BST: Blocks the defensive end unless the end slants into the C gap. If this situation occurs, BST works to the next level and blocks the strong tandem.

X: Blocks downfield.

QB: Takes a slight jab step with his right foot as he receives the snap. Reverse pivots on his right foot and softly tosses the ball to the wingback.

TB: Fakes the tailback stampede.

FB: Blocks Stud.

WB: Gains depth on his first two steps, receives the toss from the quarterback, and reads the blocks of the AST and Y.

Reinforcing the Stampede Series
with Play-Action Passes

Diagrams 7-10A through 7-10C illustrate three play-action passes that are easily installed into the stampede series.

The first pass (Diagram 7-10A) takes advantage of a tailback who has the ability to throw the ball. After the quarterback pitches the ball to the tailback, he will bootleg away from the play and find a backside window. Frequently, defenses will lose sight of the quarterback and he will be wide open. The patterns of X, Y, and Z are flexible and can be adjusted depending upon the coverage. The blocking assignments for interior linemen are as follows:

- **AST:** Blocks the weak end.
- **ASG:** Blocks Mike.
- **C:** Blocks the nose.
- **BSG:** Blocks the strong tandem.
- **BST:** Blocks the strong end.

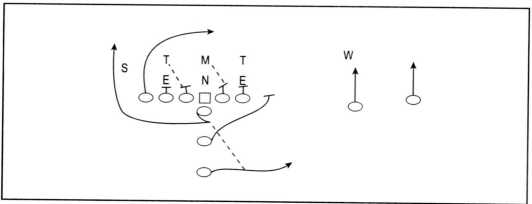

Diagram 7-10A

Diagram 7-10B illustrates a pass that is initiated from toss trey fake. Both tailback and quarterback will fake the toss trey. After faking the trey, the tailback will block the strong tandem. The fullback, X, and Z will run immediate pass routes and Y will check Stud before releasing on his outlet route. The blocking assignments for interior linemen are as follows:

- **AST:** Blocks the weak end.
- **ASG:** Blocks Mike.

- **C:** Blocks the nose.

- **BSG:** Pulls and blocks the strong tandem.

- **BST:** Blocks the strong end.

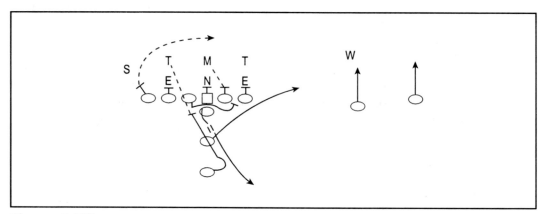

Diagram 7-10B

The last stampede play-action pass (Diagram 7-10C) is a double screen. Like the previous play, this play is also initiated from a toss trey fake. The initial blocking assignments for interior linemen are identical to those of Diagram 7-10A. After executing these assignments for three seconds, the interior linemen will release to their illustrated screen assignments. Both Y and Z will block the two tandems if these defenders drop into coverage. If the tandems blitz, they will be blocked by the BSG and fullback long enough for the quarterback to throw the ball. The fullback is responsible for blocking the weak tandem if he blitzes and then releasing for his pattern. The tailback should make a great fake and then release into his pattern.

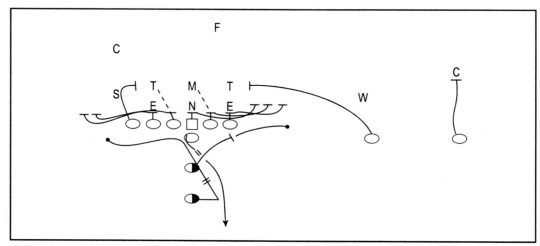

Diagram 7-10C

8

Attacking the 3-3-5 with the Option Series

I f a coach were limited to only one running play, the triple option would be his best choice because it attacks all sectors of the defense. It compels the defense to play forced assignment football, and it curtails the defense's ability to blitz. However, the biggest advantage of this play is that it almost always forces the defense into single coverage of all wide receivers. Advocates of the spread offense explain all of the overly complex tactics that they employ for the sole purpose of creating single coverage of one wide receiver, but the game isn't as complex as some people try to make it. If a coach really wants to throw the ball into single coverage, all he has to do is install one running play into his offense: the triple option. Even a bastardized version of the play that misleads the defense into believing that they must defend the triple option will often accomplish this goal.

Fullback Dive

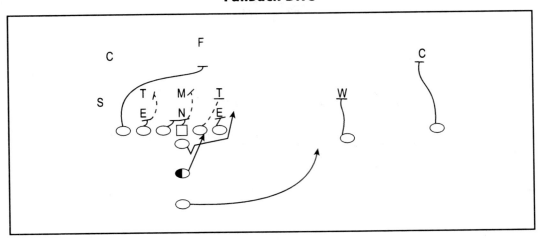

Diagram 8-1

Coaching Points: This play is a predetermined give to the fullback. After the handoff, the quarterback and tailback will carry out an option fake.

Y: Blocks downfield.

AST: Zones with the ASG. Attacks the outside breastplate of the defensive end blocks this defender unless he slants inside. If this occurs, AST will block the weak tandem.

ASG: Zones with the AST. Attacks the inside breastplate of the defensive end blocks this defender if he slants inside. Otherwise ASG works to the second level and blocks the weak tandem.

C: Zones with the BSG. Steps with his right foot and attacks the playside breastplate of the nose. Blocks the nose if the nose slants into the attackside A gap. Otherwise, the center will work to the next level and block Mike.

BSG: Zones with the center. Attacks the near breastplate of the nose and blocks the nose unless the defender slants into the attackside A gap. If this situation occurs, BSG will block Mike.

BST: Blocks the defensive end unless the end slants into the C gap. If this situation occurs, BST works to the next level and blocks the strong tandem

X: Blocks downfield.

QB: Steps with his right foot at about a 45-degree angle. Extends the ball and meshes with the fullback. Rides the fullback during the handoff.

TB: Fakes the option.

FB: Steps toward the outside foot of the ASG. Receives than handoff and explodes through the hole.

Z: Blocks downfield.

Quarterback Option

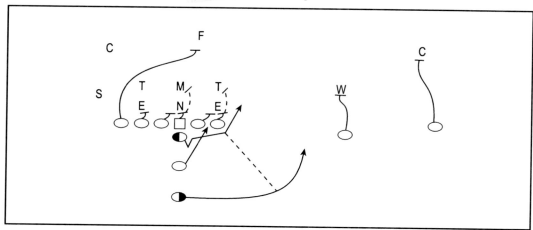

Diagram 8-2

Coaching Points: Because all of the defenders in the box are blocked, the quarterback will not actually option a specific defender. He will simply fake to the fullback and keep the ball. If the quarterback encounters a pursuing defender, he will then pitch the ball to the tailback.

Y: Blocks downfield.

AST: Zones with the ASG. Attacks the outside breastplate of the defensive end. Blocks this defender if he slants outside. Otherwise, AST will block the weak tandem.

ASG: Zones with the AST. Attacks the inside breastplate of the defensive end. Blocks this defender unless he slants outside. If this situation occurs, ASG works to the second level and blocks the weak tandem.

C: Zones with the BSG. Steps weakside and attacks the playside breastplate of the nose. Blocks the nose if the nose slants into the attackside A gap. Otherwise, the center will work to the next level and block Mike.

BSG: Zones with the center. Attacks the near breastplate of the nose and blocks the nose unless the defender slants into the attackside A gap. If this occurs, BSG will block Mike.

BST: Blocks the defensive end unless the end slants into the C gap. If this situation occurs, BST works to the next level and blocks the strong tandem.

X: Blocks downfield.

QB: Steps with his right foot at about a 45-degree angle. Extends the ball and meshes with the fullback. Rides the fullback into the line by stepping with his left foot. After the fake, the quarterback will attempt to work uphill as he comes down the line. He will keep the ball unless he encounters a pursuing defender

TB: Maintains a proper pitch relationship with the quarterback (approximately four yards in front of the quarterback). Expects a bad pitch and is prepared to recover it.

FB: Makes a convincing fake that enables him to get tackled.

Z: Blocks downfield.

Variations of the Inside Veer

Diagrams 8-3A through 8-3E illustrate five variations of the inside veer. Diagram 8-3A illustrates a variation in which the quarterback will option the weakside stack (the weak end and weak tandem). As he makes his first step, the quarterback will immediately read the reaction of the two stacked defenders. One of these defenders should close inside and tackle the fullback. If neither defender closes inside, the quarterback will give the ball to the fullback. If one of these defenders tackles the fullback, the quarterback will fake to the fullback, get upfield as quickly as possible, and pitch the ball only if he encounters defensive pursuit. The AST plays a key role in this play. He will step with his outside foot and attack the outside breastplate of the defensive end. If the end closes inside to tackle the fullback, the AST will continue to work to the next level and block the weak tandem. If the defensive end does not close inside, the AST will block him and prevent him from playing the quarterback. The center/BST scoop of the nose is another key ingredient to the success of this play. If these two linemen are not capable of sealing off the nose, the offense must resort to the next variation.

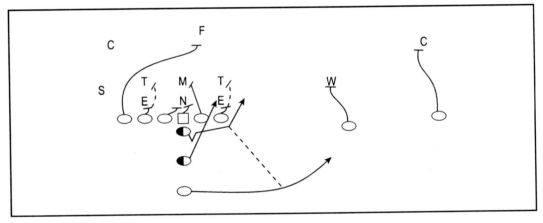

Diagram 8-3A

Diagram 8-3B illustrates the true triple option. As with the previous play, the quarterback will read the two stacked defenders. If neither defender attacks the fullback, the quarterback will hand the ball to the fullback. If one of these defenders attacks the fullback, the quarterback will keep the ball and read the next defender. The quarterback should aggressively force the second defender to quickly commit to attacking either himself or the tailback. If the second defender attacks the quarterback, the quarterback will pitch the ball; otherwise, he will keep it.

Diagram 8-3C illustrates a predetermined keep/pitch option. Since everyone is blocked, this play really isn't an option. The quarterback will simply fake to the fullback and the keep the ball. The quarterback will pitch the ball only if he encounters defensive penetration or quick pursuit.

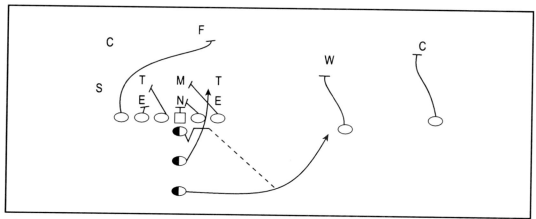

Diagram 8-3B

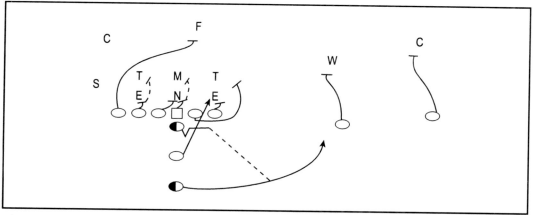

Diagram 8-3C

Diagrams 8-3D and 8-3E illustrate two schemes that exploit the tango read. In Diagram 8-3D, the AST is blocking inside, which will cause a defensive end (who is tango reading with the weak tandem) to close inside and tackle the fullback. Upon reading the AST's block, the weak tandem will scrape outside and attempt to tackle the quarterback, but because he is being blocked by the slotback, the weak tandem should not be successful. In Diagram 8-3E, the AST is blocking the defensive end. This key will cause a tango-reading weak tandem to tackle the fullback. Upon reading the AST's block, the defensive end will attempt to tackle the quarterback, but since the end is being double-teamed, he should not be successful. Furthermore, both schemes are enhanced by the utilization of a tight slot formation, which creates a wide funnel for the quarterback to run through.

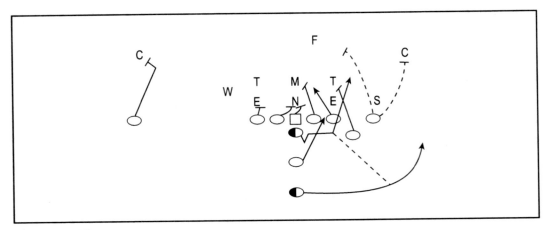

Diagram 8-3D

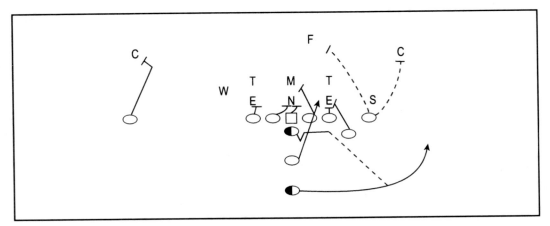

Diagram 8-3E

Speed Option

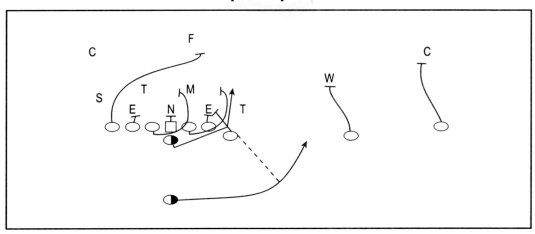

Diagram 8-4

Coaching Points: A trips formation will force most 3-3-5 teams to get out of their base alignment and into a variation of the 3-4. This adjustment often causes the defense to become unsound versus the speed option toward the three-receiver side of the formation.

Y: Blocks downfield.

AST: Double-teams with the defensive end with the slotback.

ASG: Pulls and blocks Mike.

C: Steps with his playside foot and blocks the nose. Attacks the defender's outside breastplate and hooks him in.

BSG: Pulls and cuts off the strong tandem's pursuit.

BST: Blocks the defensive end.

X: Blocks downfield.

QB: Drop steps and then comes down the line and options the weak tandem. The quarterback should be aggressive and force the strong tandem to quickly commit.

TB: Maintains a good pitch relationship with the quarterback. Is prepared to recover a bad pitch.

FB: Lines up in the slot and double-teams the defensive end with the AST.

Z: Blocks the Whip.

Trap Option

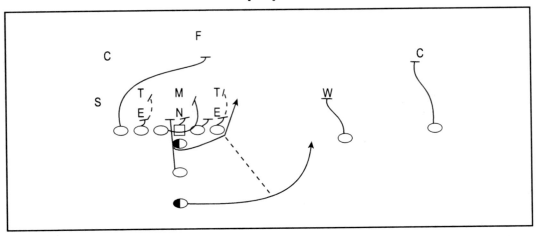

Diagram 8-5

Coaching Points: This play complements the gut series. Although not a true trap option, this play can be installed as a predetermined pitch. It can also be implemented as a predetermined quarterback keep with the quarterback having the option of pitching the ball if he encounters defensive penetration.

Y: Blocks downfield.

AST: Zones with the ASG. Attacks the outside breastplate of the defensive end and blocks this defender if he slants outside. Otherwise, AST will block the weak tandem.

ASG: Zones with the AST. Attacks the inside breastplate of the defensive end and blocks this defender unless he slants outside. If this situation occurs, ASG works to the second level and blocks the weak tandem.

C: Blocks the nose. Steps with his right foot and attacks the playside breastplate of the defender.

BSG: Pulls playside and blocks Mike.

BST: Blocks the defensive end unless the end slants into the C gap. If this situation occurs, BST works to the next level and blocks the strong tandem.

X: Blocks downfield.

QB: Reverse pivots and quickly attacks the perimeter. Does not fake to the fullback. It is the fullback's responsibility to sell the fake.

TB: Maintains a good pitch relationship with the quarterback. Is prepared to recover a bad pitch.

FB: Fakes the trap by slapping his right elbow with his left hand. Blocks nose if the defender slants into the backside A gap. Otherwise, player will block the strong tandem.

Z: Lines up in the slot and blocks Whip.

Counter Option

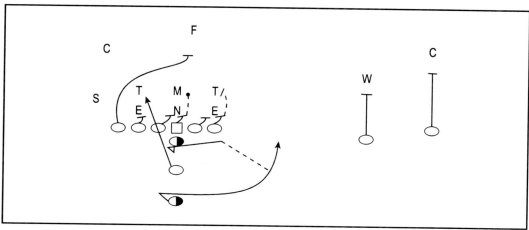

Diagram 8-6

Coaching Points: Like the trap option, this play can be installed as a predetermined pitch. It can also be implemented as a predetermined quarterback keep with the quarterback having the option of pitching the ball if he encounters defensive penetration. The misdirection makes it easier for the ASG and AST to execute their zone scheme.

Y: Blocks downfield.

AST: Zones with the ASG. Attacks the outside breastplate of the defensive end and blocks this defender if he slants outside. Otherwise, AST will block the weak tandem.

ASG: Zones with the AST. Attacks the inside breastplate of the defensive end blocks this defender unless he slants outside. If this occurs, ASG works to the second level and blocks the weak tandem.

C: Zones with the BSG. Steps weakside and attacks the playside breastplate of the nose. Blocks the nose if the nose slants into the attackside A gap. Otherwise, the center will work to the next level and block Mike.

BSG: Zones with the center. Attacks the near breastplate of the nose and blocks the nose unless the defender slants into the attackside A gap. If this situation occurs, BSG will block Mike.

BST: Blocks the defensive end.

X: Blocks downfield.

QB: Steps with his left foot at about a 45-degree angle. Extends the ball and meshes with the fullback. Does not have time to ride the fullback toward the line. Pivots on his left foot and attacks the perimeter.

TB: Maintains a good pitch relationship with the quarterback. Is prepared to recover a bad pitch.

FB: Fakes the dive by slapping his right elbow with his left hand and then blocks the strong tandem.

Z: Lines up in the slot and blocks the Whip.

Midline Option

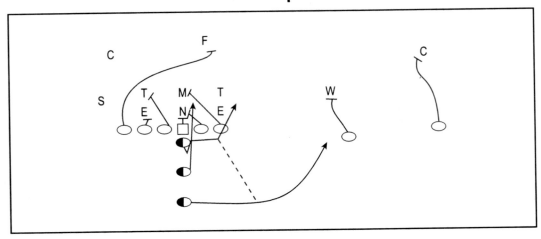

Diagram 8-7

Coaching Points: This play forces the one of the weak stacked defenders to immediately commit himself to the dive.

Y: Blocks downfield.

AST: Blocks Mike

ASG: Double-teams the nose with the center unless Mike blitzes into the backside A gap. If this situation occurs, ASG will block the nose by himself.

C: Double-teams the defensive end with Y unless Mike blitzes into the backside A gap. If this situation occurs, the center will release pressure from the nose and block the Mike.

BSG: Blocks the strong tandem.

BST: Blocks the defensive end.

X: Blocks downfield.

QB: Drop steps with his right foot and reads the weak stack (both the weak end and weak tandem) as he rides the fullback. If neither stacked defender attacks the fullback, the quarterback will give the ball to the fullback. If one of the stacked defenders attacks the fullback, the quarterback will keep or pitch the ball, depending upon the reaction of the other stacked defender.

TB: Maintains a good pitch relationship with the quarterback. Is prepared to recover a bad pitch.

FB: Runs the midline course directly into the attackside A gap. Either receives the ball or blocks Mike.

Z: Lines up in the slot and blocks the Whip.

Load Option

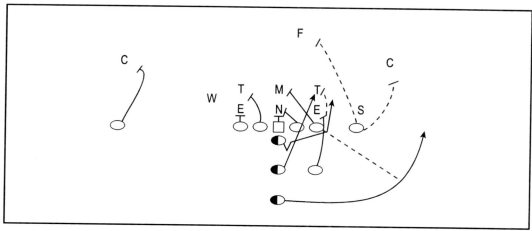

Diagram 8-8

Coaching Points: The load tactic can be used to enhance the triple option or the midline option. When the play is run from a power I formation that employs a nasty split, Stud will be forced to line up outside of the tight end, which creates a big alley for the quarterback keep. If Stud lines up inside of the tight end, the defense becomes vulnerable to a quick pitch to the halfback.

Y: Blocks downfield. Can be assigned to block either the free safety or the strong cornerback.

AST: Blocks Mike.

ASG: Double-teams the nose with the center unless Mike blitzes into the backside A gap. If this situation occurs, ASG will block the nose by himself.

C: Double-teams the defensive end with Y unless Mike blitzes into the backside A gap. If this occurs, the center will release pressure from the nose and block Mike.

BSG: Blocks the strong tandem.

BST: Blocks the defensive end.

X: Blocks downfield.

QB: Steps as he would for the triple option. Reads the two weak stacked defenders as he rides the fullback. Keeps or gives the ball, depending upon the reaction of the stacked defenders.

TB: Maintains a good pitch relationship with the quarterback. Is prepared to recover a bad pitch.

FB: Runs the triple option course. Receives the ball or blocks downfield.

HB: Steps at the outside foot of the AST and blocks the C gap defender (defender assigned to tackle the quarterback). HB will block the tandem if the end tackles the fullback, or he will block the end if the tandem tackles the fullback.

Outside Veer

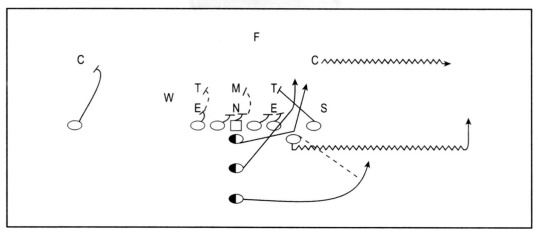

Diagram 8-9

Coaching Points: By running this play from a tight slot and then sending the slotback into motion, the offense creates a big alley for both the fullback give and the quarterback keep.

Y: Blocks the strong tandem.

AST: Double-teams the defensive end with the ASG. Attacks the outside breastplate of the defensive end drives him backwards.

ASG: Double-teams the defensive end with the AST. Attacks the inside breastplate of the defensive end drives him backwards.

C: Zones with the BSG. Steps weakside and attacks the playside breastplate of the nose. Blocks the nose if the nose slants into the attackside A gap. Otherwise, the center will work to the next level and block Mike.

BSG: Zones with the center. Attacks the near breastplate of the nose and blocks the nose unless the defender slants into the attackside A gap. If this situation occurs, BSG will block Mike.

BST: Blocks the defensive end unless the end slants into the C gap. If this situation occurs, BST works to the next level and blocks the strong tandem.

X: Blocks downfield.

QB: Pushes off his left foot and drives down the line to a point directly behind the AST. Reads Stud's reaction and either gives or keeps.

TB: Maintains a proper pitch relationship with the quarterback (approximately four yards in front of the quarterback). Expects a bad pitch and is prepared to recover it.

FB: Drives to the outside leg of the AST. Receives the handoff or continues downfield and blocks the free safety.

SB: Lines up in the slot, goes in motion, and blocks downfield.

Quarterback Counter

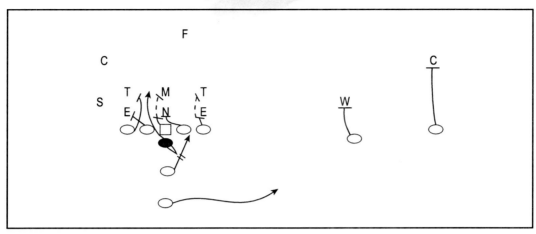

Diagram 8-10

Coaching Points: Most plays in the option series are directed outside of the guards and into the perimeter. This play gives the offense a quick hitting play inside of the guards. Often the stacked linebackers will align themselves deeper versus option offenses in an attempt to improve their tango reads. This play takes advantage of the depth of their alignment.

Y: Blocks downfield.

AST: Folds inside and blocks the weak tandem. If the weak tandem blitzes into the C gap, AST will block downfield.

ASG: Blocks the defensive end.

C: Zones with the BSG. Attacks the playside breastplate of the nose. Blocks the nose if the nose slants into the attackside A gap. Otherwise, the center will work to the next level and block Mike.

BSG: Zones with the center. Attacks the near breastplate of the nose and blocks the nose unless the defender slants into the attackside A gap. If this occurs, BSG will block Mike.

BST: Blocks the end or the first defender that shows in the B gap.

X: Blocks downfield.

QB: Steps as he would on the triple option, but does not ride the fullback. After quickly faking to the fullback, the quarterback will push off his right foot and immediately burst through the hole.

TB: Runs his pitch course.

FB: Fakes the dive. Makes a good fake by slapping his left elbow with his right hand.

Z: Lines up in the slot and blocks Whip.

Augmenting the Option Series with Play-Action Passes

Play-action passes are easily installed into the option series. This section will cover the two most effective structures into which various pattern combinations can be integrated.

The first structure is illustrated in Diagram 8-11A. This structure affords the offense maximum protection of the quarterback. When this structure is employed, X, Z, and the tailback will run pass patterns. Because all three receivers are running their patterns toward the same side of the formation, this structure favors both flood and rub patterns. The tight end will block Stud if he rushes and run a designated outlet pattern if Stud drops into coverage. The fullback will fake the dive and check the weak tandem before running his outlet route. The interior linemen's responsibilities are as follows:

- **AST:** Blocks the weak end.
- **ASG:** Blocks Mike.
- **C:** Blocks the nose.
- **BSG:** Blocks the strong tandem.
- **BST:** Blocks the strong end.

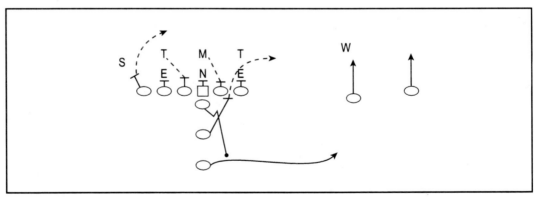

Diagram 8-11A

The second structure (Diagram 8-11B) is similar to the first with the following exceptions:

- The quarterback will pitch the ball to the tailback and the tailback will throw the pass.
- The tight end becomes a primary receiver.
- The fullback doesn't have an outlet route.
- The quarterback will assist in protecting the C gap after pitching the ball to the tailback.

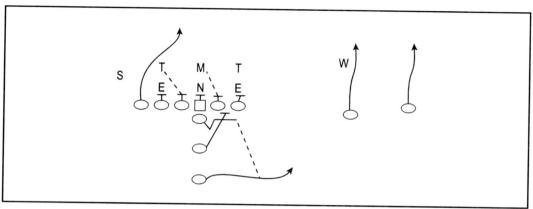

Diagram 8-11B

Part 3:
Attacking the 3-3-5 with the Pass

9

Seventeen Ways to Enhance the Efficiency of Your Pass Offense

#1: Have the Quarterback Set Up Behind the Tackle

The following are three reasons why it is advantageous to have one's quarterback set up behind the tackle (five- and seven-step drops) rather than having him drop straight back. First, it strengthens the quarterback's arm to the wideside of the field. Over 75 percent of the plays in high school and college football originate from a spot on or near one of the hash marks. Unlike professional football, where the ball pretty much stays in the middle of the field, high school and college teams have to deal with both a wideside and a shortside of the field. By having his quarterback set up behind the tackle toward the wideside of the field, a coach can significantly strengthen his quarterback's arm.

Second, it enhances pass protection. Quarterbacks who drop straight back provide two good pass rush lanes for defensive linemen who are aligned on the center and guards. Quarterbacks who set up behind the Tackle run away from one-half of their pass rush. They also dictate to the defense which gap is the most desirable pass rush lane. This helps offensive linemen because they can favor this lane and quickly wash out defenders that choose the least desirable pass rush lane.

Third, it creates misdirection in the passing game. Because defenses get accustomed to seeing the quarterback throw toward the direction of his drop, throwback patterns usually gain big yardage.

: Use Max Protection versus the Zone Blitz

In the old days, defenders who lined up in three-point stances were pass rushers and the players who lined up in two point stances were either pass rushers (if they blitzed) or coverage players. Today, every player aligned in the box is both a potential pass rusher and a coverage player. The zone blitz has therefore rewritten the rules of pass protection by holding the offense accountable for blocking all of the defenders aligned in or near the box. Max protection has thus become the preferred method of protecting a quarterback who is dropping five or seven steps. Quarterbacks who have been coached to rely on hot reads to as the exclusive panacea for dealing with the zone blitz often find themselves dumping the ball off to a hot receiver and gaining only four or five yards in a long yardage situation and then being forced to punt.

Old school max protection schemes, similar to the one illustrated in Diagram 9-1, are the most effective way of dealing with the zone blitz. Because the free safety is playing in the center of the formation, a strong probability is created that either Stud or the strong tandem will be forced to drop into coverage. If this were to occur, the tailback would simply block whichever defender rushes. If both Stud and the strong tandem were to rush, the strong end would be forced to drop into coverage. In this scenario, the tackle would block the strong tandem and the tailback would block Stud.

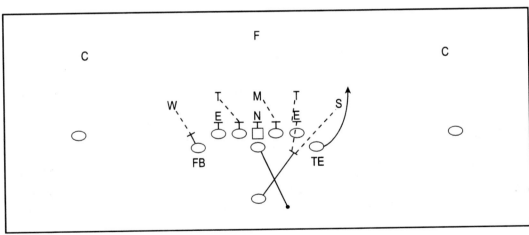

Diagram 9-1

#3: Beat the Blitz with Three-Step Drop Pass Routes

Another tactic versus a blitzing defense is to have the quarterback throw timed three-step patterns (fade, hitch, out, slant, etc.). These patterns are thrown so quickly that it is extremely difficult for the defense to get to the quarterback before he unloads the ball.

#4: Use Screen Passes, Shovel Passes, and Draws

Screen passes are an effective tactic versus an overly aggressive blitzing defense. Shovel passes and draws are extremely potent versus three- and four-man pass rushes that feature quick dropping linebackers. All three tactics should be a vital part of every offensive attack.

#5: Bunch or Stack Receivers versus Man Coverage

Receivers can be stacked or bunched in both compressed and spread formations. Natural rubs or meshes are created when receivers run crossing routes so close to one another that they almost rub against one another. This frequently results in defenders bumping into one another as they attempt to cover their assigned receiver. Bunching and stacking receivers creates an extraordinary burden for man coverage. Furthermore, when three or more receivers are bunched or stacked in spread formations, the defense is greatly limited in its ability to disrupt timed pass routes because only one of the receivers is aligned on the line of scrimmage. This strategy is particularly effective at the goal line.

#6: Use Motion to Prevent the Bump

It is extremely difficult for any pass defender (defensive back or linebacker) to jam a moving target at the line of scrimmage. Attempting to jam a motioned receiver frequently results in the defender missing his jam, or overextending and loosing his balance.

#7: Create a Mismatch by Stemming the Tight End and then Employing Backfield Motion

This tactic is frequently used against a 3-3-5 that has two different types of athlete playing outside linebacker. One type is the Stud (S). This player is primarily a linebacker and will always align on the side of the tight end. He is big, tough, and physical. The other outside linebacker is the adjuster (A). The adjuster is usually a hybrid who is 50 percent linebacker and 50 percent defensive back. The adjuster will play opposite the tight end and is a much better cover player than the Stud; he is also less effective versus the run. In Diagram 9-2, the offense initially aligns the tight end right and then stems him left. Frequently, the defense views a tight end stem as an annoyance; therefore, it will not flip-flop its outside linebackers because it assumes that if it pays minimum attention to the stem that the offense will stop doing it. When the offense motions its fullback (or tailback) immediately following the stem, it creates a mismatch by isolating a running back in a one-on-one situation versus the Stud.

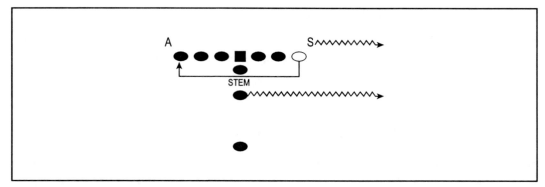

Diagram 9-2

#8: Rapidly Shift Formation Strength Followed by Backfield Motion

A slowly executed formation shift usually has minimal effect on a defense, but a quick shift followed by motion can create serious havoc with the most sophisticated defense. Diagram 9-3 illustrates a shift in which the offense initially lined up in a slot right formation. At the quarterback's command, the slotback moves to a halfback position and the fullback moves to a slotback position. After waiting one second after the shift, the tailback then goes into (full speed) motion. This rapid shift followed by motion, not only changes formation strength, but also forces the defense to adjust to a trips formation.

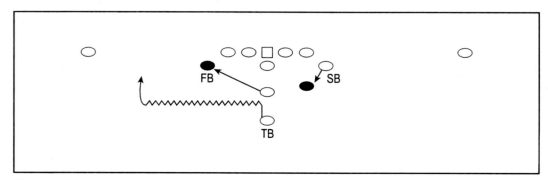

Diagram 9-3

#9: Use Sight Adjustments versus Coverage Disguise

Defensive secondaries usually do an excellent job of disguising their coverages. Even when passes are called at the line of scrimmage, the offense will often find that the pattern that was called, one that looked good before the ball was snapped, no longer looks good versus a disguised coverage. When this occurs, both the quarterback and the receivers must be able to read the coverage and change the pattern as the play is in progress. This tactic is referred to as sight adjustment. Any sophisticated passing attack will have sight adjustments built into its pass routes. For sight adjustments to become effective, they must become innate, which can only be achieved with constant practice. The quarterback and receivers must continually be confronted by post-snap reads that differ from the pre-snap read.

#10: Create Vertical Stretch of Zone Coverages

By vertically stretching a zone, an offense is able to exploit it with high-low patterns. High-low patterns are attained by running two receivers into the same zone. One receiver will run a deep route; the other receiver will run a short route. The defender assigned to cover the zone must make a choice as to which receiver he will cover. Diagram 9-4 illustrates an excellent pattern that high-lows the backside hook zone. The quarterback will simply read the defender responsible for covering this zone and either throw the ball to the split end or tight end. Any zone in a zone defense can be high-lowed. When attempting to high-low a zone, it is important to remember that the two receivers should be at least 10 yards apart; otherwise, the isolated defender will probably be able to cover both receivers. Also, the two receivers should not be positioned in the same throwing lane.

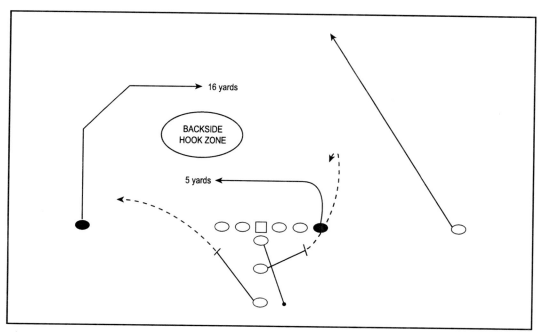

Diagram 9-4

#11: Create Horizontal Stretch of Zone Coverages

Zone can be stretched horizontally to their max by running two receivers along or into the diametrical perimeters of the zone. This makes it extremely difficult for the isolated defender assigned to the zone to cover both receivers. By stretching a zone horizontally, the offense is able to exploit it with patterns that attack the seams of the zone. Diagram 9-5 illustrates a post pattern that isolates the deep middle of a three-deep zone.

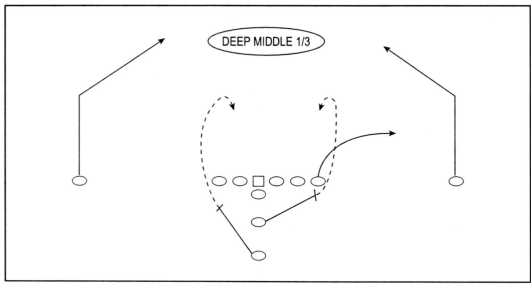

Diagram 9-5

#12: Simplify the Quarterback's Read

Few high school quarterbacks are experienced enough to read the entire field. Have the quarterback zero in on a single defender or specific area of the field simplifies his thought process and results in better decisions and greater efficiency.

#13: Throw Timed Pass Routes

Timing is a key element in any successful passing attack. When a timed route is thrown, the receiver will not see the quarterback throw the ball; the ball will be thrown as the receiver makes his break. It is almost impossible for a defender (particularly a backpedaling defensive back) to react quickly enough to stop the completion of a precisely thrown timed route. It is therefore extremely vital that timing is achieved between the quarterback and his receivers. Although all of the routes in a particular pass pattern may not require timing, at least one or two of the routes will.

#14: Throw Pick Patterns

Although picks are illegal in the NFL, they're still legal in high school and college football, provided the ball is caught behind the line of scrimmage. The bubble screen (Diagram 9-6A) is an example of a pick pattern. Pick patterns can also be thrown to running backs. Diagram 9-6B illustrates an example of a screen pattern in which the slot receiver is cracking on the defender assigned to cover the fullback (either the weak tandem or Mike).

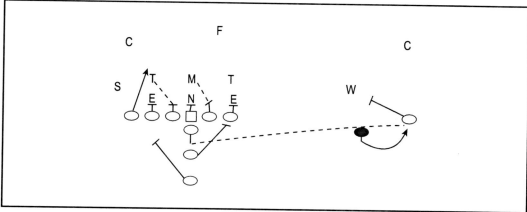

Diagram 9-6A

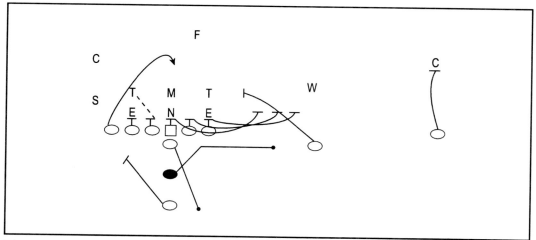

Diagram 9-6B

#15: Use Counter-Reactive Pass Routes

A counter-reactive pass route is a precisely-timed route that contradicts and thereby negates the technique used by a defender. A counter-reactive route is effective versus both man and zone coverage because it exploits a specific technique used by a defender and does not concern itself with the overall coverage. A hitch route, for example, is a counter-reactive pass route because it negates the backpedal technique used by the cornerback.

#16: Use Counter-Punch Pass Patterns

A counter-punch pass pattern negates a defender's reaction to a pattern by having a receiver run a pattern, stop momentarily, and then run a second pattern. The hitch-and-go pattern is an example of a counter-punch pattern.

#17: Use Play-Action Passes

Play-action passes nullify a linebacker's and/or a defensive back's reaction to a pass by freezing the defender with a run-action fake. Play-action passes are most effective when they are used in situations when the offense would normally run the football. They should not be used when the defense expects the offense to pass.

10

Ensuring Maximum Pass Protection versus 3-3-5 Blitzes

It is the quarterback's responsibility to be able to recognize the defensive alignment and set the protection in a manner that will ensure that all defenders aligned in the box are blocked. A twins formation makes it extremely difficult for the defense to disguise its coverage and thus simplifies the quarterback's task. In Diagrams 10-1A and 10-1B, Whip is walked off and the free safety is not in a position to cover the slot receiver. The defense is therefore capable of doing one of three things.: play cover 3, play cover 1, or blitz either the strong corner or free safety. Versus the first two scenarios, the quarterback can release either the tailback or fullback as one of the three primary pass receivers and be assured of maximum protection. A very important point to mention is that whenever a running back or tight end is assigned to block in the protection scheme, the player will only block if his assigned defender rushes. If the defender drops into coverage, the running back or tight end will run an outlet route.

Versus a secondary blitz, the quarterback should be instructed to audible to a sweep away from the direction of the secondary blitz. In other words, if the strong corner were to blitz, the quarterback would call a sweep toward the twin receivers; if the free safety were to blitz, the quarterback would call the sweep toward the tight end. Sometimes, the defense does a great job of disguising its secondary blitz and the quarterback is not able to audible to a sweep. When this occurs, the quarterback should use whichever running back is being released into the pattern as a hot receiver, try to scramble away from the blitz, and throw the ball into the dirt and waste the down.

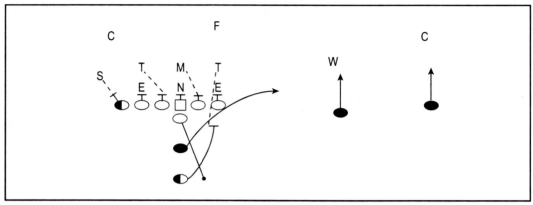

Diagram 10-1A

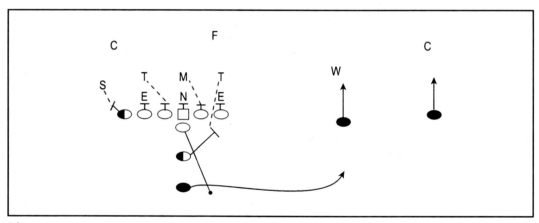

Diagram 10-1B

When Whip is in a position to blitz and the free safety is in a position to cover the slot receiver (Diagram 10-1C), the quarterback should use maximum protection.

A deuce formation also simplifies the quarterback's task of calling a protection scheme that will insure that all defenders aligned in the box are accounted for. When using this formation, the quarterback simply reads the alignment of the free safety. If the free safety is aligned in the middle of the formation, the quarterback is free to call his protection in either direction. When the free safety is favoring one side of the formation, he is able to cover the tight end, and the defense is capable of employing either an overload or illusion blitz toward the side that the free safety is favoring. In this scenario, the quarterback would call the protection scheme illustrated in Diagram 10-2.

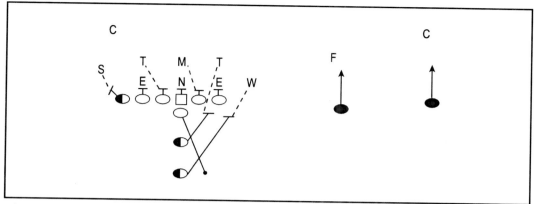

Diagram 10-1C

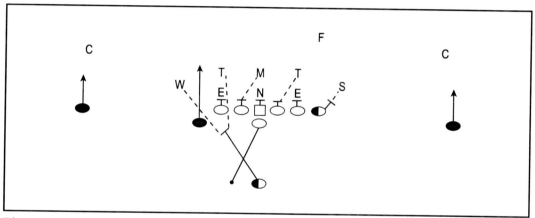

Diagram 10-2

Trips also simplifies the quarterback's task. Versus trips, most defenses will move Whip out of the box and reduce to a seven-man front. When this occurs, the quarterback will employ the protection scheme illustrated in Diagram 10-3A. Occasionally, a defense may remain in their eight-man front, play corners over, and put their free safety in a position that will enable him to cover the fullback (#3 strong). When this occurs, the quarterback will use the protection scheme illustrated in Diagram 10-3B.

The pro formation is a good formation to throw quick passes in which the quarterback takes a one- to three-step drop. It is also a safe formation to throw passes in which the quarterback takes five- and seven-step drops whenever the free safety is aligned in the middle of the formation (Diagram 10-4A). When the free safety lines up in a position to cover the tight end, however, the defense is capable of an illusion or overload blitz. In this situation, the offense takes a chance by releasing its tight end as a primary receiver. If this approach is taken, the tight end should definitely be used as a hot read. The only way that the offense can insure maximum protection in this situation is to keep its tight end in as a blocker (Diagram 10-4B).

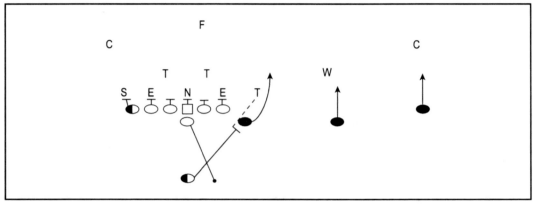

Diagram 10-3A

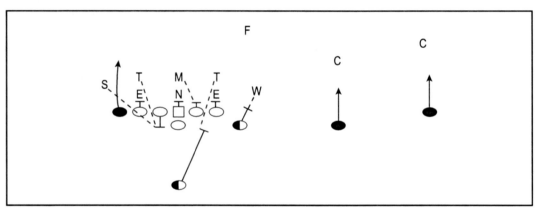

Diagram 10-3B

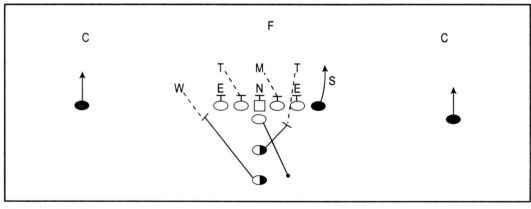

Diagram 10-4A

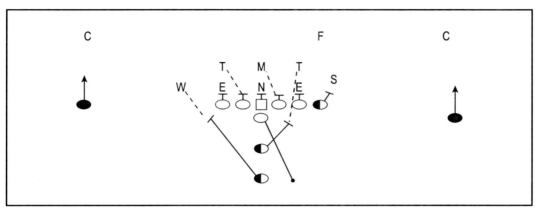

Diagram 10-4B

3-3-5 teams often align their secondary in a four-deep secondary shell versus the pro formation. When confronted by this look, the quarterback can insure maximum protection with the scheme illustrated in Diagram 10-5.

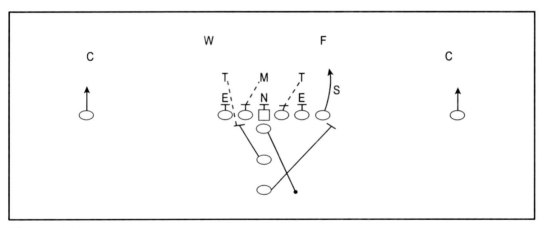

Diagram 10-5

11

Forty Great Pass Plays that Exploit 3-3-5 Pass Coverages

The purpose of this chapter is to present forty pass plays that will assault any type of pass coverage that an offense may face. Included are schemes that feature seam isolation, counter reactive, counter punch, rub, pick, and high-lows tactics.

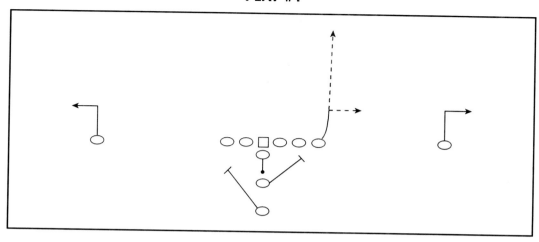

Purpose: This quick out is a counter-reactive pattern that exploits the backpedal technique of the cornerback.

Quarterback: Takes a three-step drop and throws the ball as the receiver makes his break. Throws a strike between the receiver's belt and shoulder pads. Leads the receiver toward the sideline. Drills the ball and doesn't let it hang in the air.

Flanker: Speed cuts on his fourth step. Snaps his head around and looks for the ball immediately after making his fourth step.

Tight End: Runs a quick out versus a three-deep shell. Runs a seam away from the inside linebackers versus a four-deep shell.

Split End: Speed cuts on his fourth step. Snaps his head around and looks for the ball immediately after making his fourth step.

Fullback: Blocks the strong tandem if he blitzes. Keeps the defender's hands down with a low block. Blocks C gap if the strong tandem drops into coverage.

Tailback: Blocks Whip if he blitzes. Keeps the defender's hands down with a low block.

Coaching Points: Both the flanker and split end will sight adjust to a fade route versus a cornerback jam technique. This play is not a good throw toward the wideside of the field, but it is it is an excellent throw from the middle of the field or into the boundary.

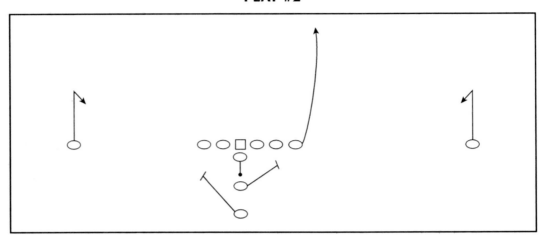

Purpose: This quick hitch is a counter-reactive pattern that exploits the backpedal technique of the cornerback.

Quarterback: Takes a three-step drop and throws the ball as the receiver makes his break. Throws the ball between the receiver's shoulder pads and waist.

Flanker: Attacks the outside shoulder of the cornerback. Takes three big steps, followed by two gather steps. Snaps his inside elbow and head around on fifth step and faces the quarterback. Keeps his head and shoulders upfield.

Tight End: Runs a seam away from the inside linebackers.

Split End: Attacks the outside shoulder of the cornerback. Takes three big steps, followed by two gather steps. Snaps his inside elbow and head around on fifth step and faces the quarterback. Keeps his head and shoulders upfield.

Fullback: Blocks the strong tandem if he blitzes. Keeps the defender's hands down with a low block. Blocks C gap if the strong tandem drops into coverage.

Tailback: Blocks Whip if he blitzes. Keeps the defender's hands down with a low block.

Coaching Points: Both the flanker and split end will sight adjust to a fade route versus a cornerback jam technique. This throw is good anywhere on the field.

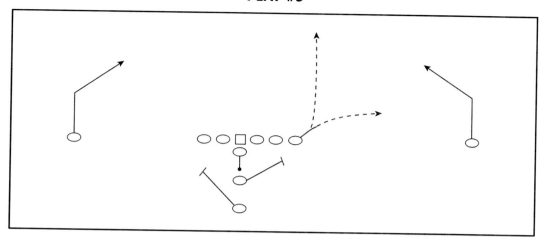

Purpose: This quick slant is a counter-reactive pattern that exploits either the backpedal technique or the outside jam technique of the cornerback.

Quarterback: Takes a three-step drop and throws the ball as the receiver makes his break. Leads the receiver with a pass below the receiver's shoulder pads. May drill the ball or soften the throw slightly depending upon the distance of the receiver's split and the tightness of the coverage.

Flanker: Attacks the outside shoulder of the cornerback. Breaks inside at a 45-degree angle on his third step. Runs under control in order to be able to adjust to a back hip throw.

Tight End: Runs a quick out versus a three-deep shell. Runs a seam away from the inside linebackers versus a four-deep shell.

Split End: Attacks the outside shoulder of the cornerback. Breaks inside at a 45-degree angle on his third step. Runs under control in order to be able to adjust to a back hip throw.

Fullback: Blocks the strong tandem if he blitzes. Keeps the defender's hands down with a low block. Blocks C gap if the strong tandem drops into coverage.

Tailback: Blocks Whip if he blitzes. Keeps the defender's hands down with a low block.

Coaching Points: Both the flanker and split end will sight adjust to a fade route versus a inside jam technique by the cornerback. This throw is good toward the wideside or from the middle of the field.

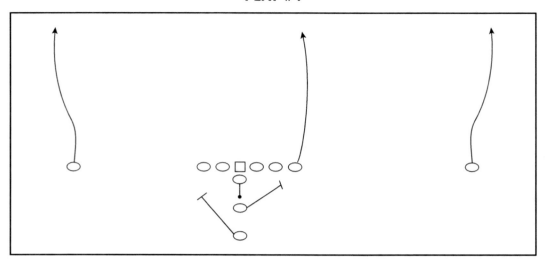

Purpose: This fade is a counter-reactive pattern that exploits the jam technique of the cornerback.

Quarterback: Takes a three-step drop and throws the ball into the open window. Uses high trajectory if the receiver beats the coverage or drills the ball if a hole exists between the cornerback and the safety. Versus cover 2, throws to the tight end if the safety playing the hash immediately jumps the flanker's route.

Flanker: Releases outside and attacks the outside shoulder of the cornerback. Always leaves at least a four-yard cushion from the sideline. Looks for the ball on his fifth step.

Tight End: Runs a seam away from the inside linebackers and slightly inside the hash. Forces a cover 2 safety to commitment.

Split End: Releases outside and attacks the outside shoulder of the cornerback. Always leaves at least a four-yard cushion from the sideline. Looks for the ball on his fifth step.

Fullback: Blocks the strong tandem if he blitzes. Keeps the defender's hands down with a low block. Blocks C gap if the strong tandem drops into coverage.

Tailback: Blocks Whip if he blitzes. Keeps the defender's hands down with a low block.

Coaching Points: Both the flanker and split end will sight adjust to a quick out, slant, or hitch route (coaches choice) versus a backpedal technique by the cornerback. This throw is great toward the wideside of the field and a good throw from the middle of the field.

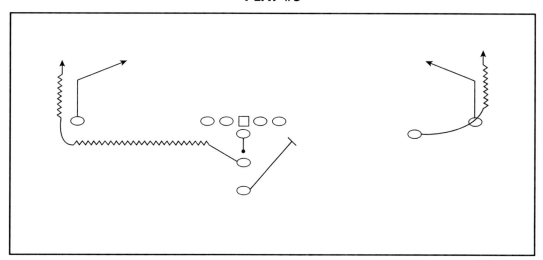

Purpose: This slant variation can be a counter-reactive pattern versus man coverage or a horizontal stretch of the flat zone. This pattern employs 20 personnel; consequently, no assignment is given for a tight end. Both split ends have the same assignment. Fullback motion is optional. Both backs may be used as blockers.

Quarterback: Takes a three-step drop and leads the receiver with a pass below the receiver's shoulder pads when throwing the slant. May use a high trajectory or drill the ball to the read receiver depending upon the cornerback's reaction

Flanker: Lines up in the slot. Stretches the underneath zone by gaining enough horizontal width to reach a landmark slightly outside of split end's initial alignment. Reads the reaction of the cornerback as he begins to gain vertical depth. If the cornerback is employing a jam technique, receiver will run a fade. If the cornerback is backpedaling, receiver will throttle down and immediately look for the ball.

Split Ends: Attacks the outside shoulder of the cornerback. Breaks inside at a 45-degree angle on his third step. Runs under control in order to be able to adjust to a back hip throw.

Fullback: Goes into quick motion and arrives at a point four yards inside of the split end when the ball is snapped. Stretches the underneath zone by continuing on a horizontal course until he reaches a landmark slightly outside of split end's initial alignment. Reads the reaction of the cornerback as he begins to gain vertical depth. If the cornerback is employing a jam technique, receiver will run a fade. If the cornerback is backpedaling, receiver will throttle down and immediately look for the ball.

Tailback: Blocks the tandem away from the fullback's motion if he blitzes. Keeps the defender's hands down with a low block. Blocks C gap if the tandem drops into coverage.

Coaching Points: No sight adjustments are necessary, other than the ones mentioned for the flanker and fullback. Good play from the hash or the middle of the field.

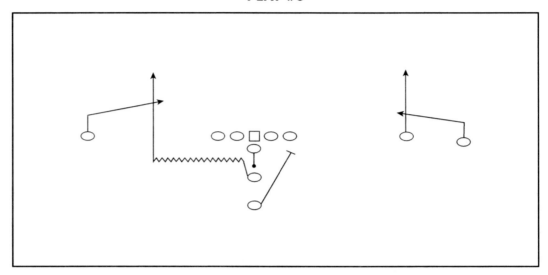

Purpose: This slant variation can be a counter-reactive pattern versus man coverage when the cornerback is deep and employing a backpedal technique and the defender covering the #2 receiver is tight and employing a jam technique. It can also be used versus a cover 3. This pattern employs 20 personnel; consequently, no assignment is given for a tight end. The split end aligned toward the flanker will be referred to as the field split end and the other split end will be referred to as the boundary split end.

Quarterback: Takes a three-step drop and reads the defender aligned in front of the #2 receiver. Throws the slant when this defender retreats, and throws a go route when this defender squats. Leads the receiver with a pass below the receiver's shoulder pads when throwing the slant. Drills the ball to the #2 receiver when throwing the go route.

Flanker: Lines up six to seven yards outside of the split end. Runs a quick slant. Breaks inside at a sharp angle on his second step.

Field Split End: Runs a go route straight up the field. Does not drift inside or outside where he can be covered by the cornerback or free safety. Immediately looks for the ball if the defender in front of him squats.

Boundary Split End: Runs a quick slant. Breaks inside at a sharp angle on his second step.

Fullback: Goes into quick motion and arrives at a point six to seven yards inside of the split end when the ball is snapped. Runs a go route straight up the field. Does not drift inside or outside where he can be covered by the cornerback or free safety. Immediately looks for the ball if the defender in front of him squats.

Tailback: Blocks the tandem away from the fullback's motion if he blitzes. Keeps the defender's hands down with a low block. Blocks C gap if the tandem drops into coverage.

Coaching Points: Both the flanker and boundary split end will sight adjust to fades versus jam techniques by the cornerbacks.

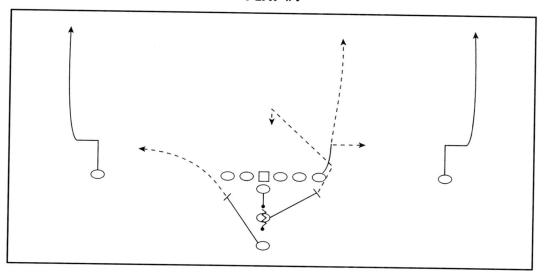

Purpose: This out-and-up pattern is a counter-punch route that exploits the cornerback's reaction to the quick out.

Quarterback: Takes a three-step drop, stops, pump fakes, and then takes two more shuffle steps. Throws the ball with high trajectory.

Flanker: Attacks the outside shoulder of the cornerback. Speed cuts on his fourth step. Sells the out by taking three more steps toward the sideline. Turns upfield on his third step and outruns the cornerback.

Tight End: Runs a quick out versus a three-deep shell. Runs a seam away from the inside linebackers versus a four-deep shell.

Split End: Attacks the outside shoulder of the cornerback. Speed cuts on his fourth step. Sells the out by taking three more steps toward the sideline. Turns upfield on his third step and outruns the cornerback

Fullback: Blocks the weak tandem if he blitzes. Run a five-yard outlet route directly in front of the center if weak tandem drops into coverage.

Tailback: Blocks Whip if he blitzes. Runs a three-yard outlet route if Whip drops into coverage.

Coaching Points: Both the flanker and split end will sight adjust to a fade route versus a cornerback jam technique. This play is an excellent throw toward the wideside of the field and a good throw from the middle of the field.

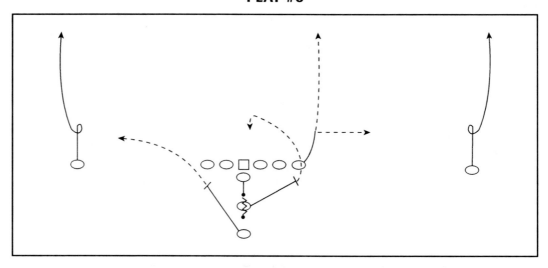

Purpose: This hitch-and-go pattern is a counter punch route that exploits the cornerback's reaction to the quick hitch.

Quarterback: Takes a three-step drop and throws the hitch if the cornerback does not bite on the route. Stops, pump fakes, takes two more shuffle steps, and throws the ball with high trajectory if the cornerback does bite on the quick hitch.

Flanker: Attacks the outside shoulder of the cornerback. Takes three big steps, followed by two gather steps. Snaps his inside elbow and head around on fifth step and faces the quarterback. Flashes his hands and numbers at the quarterback. Feels the cornerback's reaction. Turns upfield and beats the cornerback deep if the cornerback bites on the hitch. Does not turn upfield and expects the hitch to be thrown if the cornerback does not bite on the route.

Tight End: Runs a quick out versus a three-deep shell. Runs a seam away from the inside linebackers versus a four-deep shell.

Split End: Attacks the outside shoulder of the cornerback. Takes three big steps, followed by two gather steps. Snaps his inside elbow and head around on fifth step and faces the quarterback. Flashes his hands and numbers at the quarterback. Feels the cornerback's reaction. Turns upfield and beats the cornerback deep if the cornerback bites on the hitch. Does not turn upfield and expects the hitch to be thrown if the cornerback does not bite on the route.

Fullback: Blocks the strong tandem if he blitzes. Runs a five-yard outlet route directly in front of the center if the strong tandem drops into coverage.

Tailback: Blocks Whip if he blitzes. Runs a three-yard outlet route if Whip drops into coverage.

Coaching Points: Both the flanker and split end will sight adjust to a fade route versus a cornerback jam technique. This play is an excellent throw toward the wideside of the field and a good throw from the middle of the field.

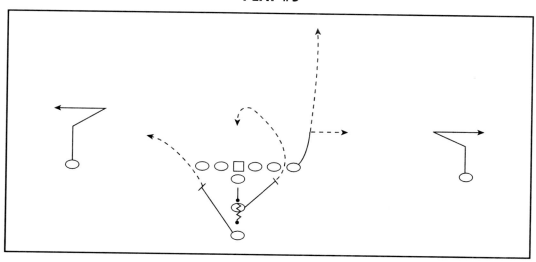

Purpose: The Whip pattern is a counter-punch route that exploits the cornerback's reaction to the quick slant.

Quarterback: Takes a three-step drop, stops, pump fakes, takes two more shuffle steps, and drills the ball between the receiver's waist and shoulders.

Flanker: Attacks the outside shoulder of the cornerback. Breaks inside at a 45-degree angle on his third step. Runs the slant for three steps. Plants on his third step and breaks flat, outside toward the sideline.

Tight End: Runs a quick out versus a three-deep shell. Runs a seam away from the inside linebackers versus a four-deep shell.

Split End: Attacks the outside shoulder of the cornerback. Breaks inside at a 45-degree angle on his third step. Runs the slant for three steps. Plants on his third step and breaks flat, outside toward the sideline.

Fullback: Blocks the strong tandem if he blitzes. Run a five-yard outlet route directly in front of the center if the strong tandem drops into coverage.

Tailback: Blocks Whip if he blitzes. Runs a three-yard outlet route if Whip drops into coverage.

Coaching Points: Both the flanker and split end will sight adjust to a fade route versus a cornerback jam technique. This throw is good from the middle of the field.

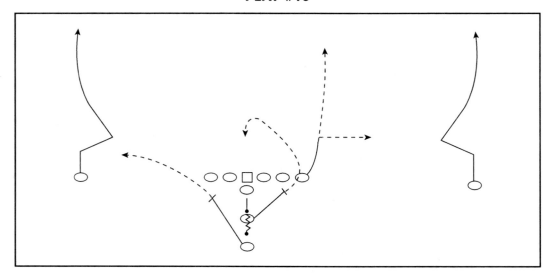

Purpose: The slant-and-go pattern is a counter-punch route that exploits the cornerback's reaction to the quick slant.

Quarterback: Takes a three-step drop, stops, pump fakes, and then takes two more shuffle steps. Throws the ball with high trajectory.

Flanker: Attacks the outside shoulder of the cornerback. Breaks inside at a 45-degree angle on his third step. Runs the slant for three steps. Plants on his third step and beats the cornerback deep.

Tight End: Runs a quick out versus a three-deep shell. Runs a seam away from the inside linebackers versus a four-deep shell.

Split End: Attacks the outside shoulder of the cornerback. Breaks inside at a 45-degree angle on his third step. Runs the slant for three steps. Plants on his third step and beats the cornerback deep.

Fullback: Blocks the strong tandem if he blitzes. Runs a five-yard outlet route directly in front of the center if the strong tandem drops into coverage.

Tailback: Blocks Whip if he blitzes. Runs a three-yard outlet route if Whip drops into coverage

Coaching Points: Both the flanker and split end will sight adjust to a fade route versus a cornerback jam technique. This play is a good throw from the middle of the field and an excellent throw toward the wideside of the field.

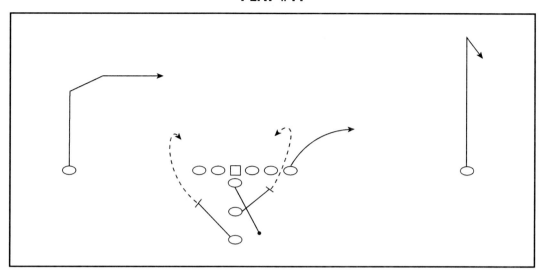

Purpose: This pattern features two of the hardest patterns in football to cover, the comeback and dig routes. This pattern is very versatile and easily adapts to play-action schemes.

Quarterback: Reads Stud. If Stud blitzes or immediately runs to one (the flanker), quarterback will stop on his fifth step and dump the ball off to the tight end. Otherwise, the quarterback will take a seven-step drop and drill the ball to the flanker. It is important that the quarterback's throw is targeted at the flanker's numbers and that the throw brings the flanker back toward the line of scrimmage.

Flanker: Attacks the outside shoulder of the cornerback. Sells the go route. Plants on his inside foot at 16 yards, turns toward the sideline, and stems back towards the ball.

Tight End: Reads Stud as he runs a quick five-yard out. If Stud blitzes, tight end is the quarterback's hot read, and he should immediately look for the ball. If Stud runs to one and ignores the tight end, tight end will look for the ball when he arrives at his five-yard landmark. It is important that tight end runs diagonally as he gains vertical depth; otherwise, the strong tandem will be able to cover him.

Split End: Runs a dig route. Attacks the outside shoulder of the cornerback as he runs vertically for 10 yards. At 10 yards, receiver will break toward the post for five more yards. At 15 yards, the receiver will flatten and run perpendicular to the line of scrimmage.

Fullback: Blocks the strong tandem if he blitzes. If strong tandem drops into coverage, fullback will check Stud. If both defenders drop into coverage, fullback will run a five-yard hook route.

Tailback: Blocks Whip if he blitzes. If Whip drops into coverage, tailback will run a five-yard hook route.

Coaching Points: The quarterback will read Stud and not concern himself with the dig route. The eye in the sky will alert the quarterback that the defense is ignoring this route when it is open.

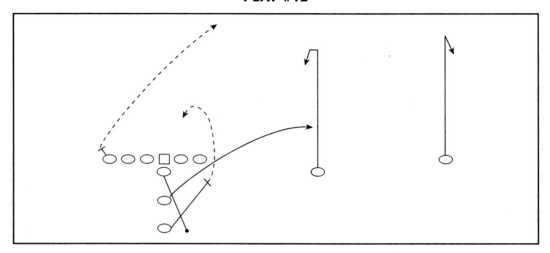

Purpose: This versatile pattern is effective versus both man and zone coverage. It is difficult for man coverage because the comeback route is extremely difficult to cover with any man-to-man technique except trail. The pattern is also difficult for zone because it high-lows the curl zone and puts an additional receiver in the out zone.

Quarterback: Takes a seven-step drop as he reads Whip and the weakside corner. Throws the comeback versus man or quarters. Versus a three-deep zone has the option of reading the high-low or throwing the comeback. Should stick with the high-low versus a two-deep zone.

Flanker: Runs a comeback-curl. Attacks Whip's outside shoulder as he releases outside and works to a depth of 16 yards. Snaps his head and inside elbow as he turns toward the quarterback. Shows the quarterback his hands and numbers as he works back toward the quarterback or inside to an open window.

Tight End: Blocks Stud if he blitzes. If Stud drops into coverage, tight end runs directly at the free safety.

Split End: Attacks the outside shoulder of the cornerback. Sells the go route. Plants on his inside foot at 16 yards, turns toward the sideline, and stems back towards the ball.

Fullback: Releases into the flats. Works diagonally until he reaches a vertical depth of three to five yards.

Tailback: Blocks the weak tandem if he blitzes. If weak tandem drops into coverage, tailback will run a five-yard hook route.

Coaching Points: The pattern adapts well to play-action schemes.

PLAY #13

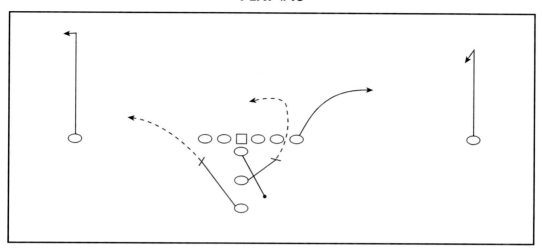

Purpose: This out/turn in combination is a counter-reactive pattern that exploits the backpedal technique of the cornerback.

Quarterback: First checks Stud. If Stud blitzes quarterback will quickly dump the ball off to the tight end. Otherwise, the quarterback will takes a five-step drop and drill the ball to either the flanker or split end. It is vital that the quarterback throws the ball as the receiver begins his break. When throwing the in, the quarterback's target should be the flanker's numbers. When throwing the out, the quarterback's target is between the base of the split end's numbers and his hip.

Flanker: Attacks the outside shoulder of the cornerback. Sells the go route. Plants on his outside foot at 12 to 14 yards (depth depends upon the receiver's speed), snaps his head and elbow inside, turns his shoulders toward the quarterback, and stems back towards the ball.

Tight End: Reads Stud as he runs a quick five-yard out. If Stud blitzes, tight end is the quarterback's hot read, and he should immediately look for the ball. If Stud runs to one and ignores the tight end, tight end will look for the ball when he arrives at his five-yard landmark. It is important that tight end runs diagonally as he gains vertical depth; otherwise, the strong tandem will be able to cover him.

Split End: Sells the go route. At a depth of 12 to 14 yards (depth depends upon the receiver's speed), receiver gains lateral separation from the cornerback with a speed cut to the outside. It is important that he snaps his head around quickly and gets his chin pointed at the ball.

Fullback: Blocks the strong tandem if he blitzes. If strong tandem drops into coverage, fullback will check Stud. If both defenders drop into coverage, fullback will run a five-yard hook route.

Tailback: Blocks Whip if he blitzes. If Whip drops into coverage, tailback will run a three-yard out route.

Coaching Points: This pattern can be thrown from the middle of the field or from the hash. When throwing it from the hash, the tight end and flanker should be set to the wideside of the field. Both the flanker and split end will adjust their routes to fades versus a cornerback jam technique.

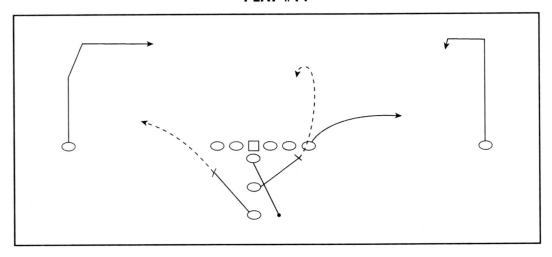

Purpose: This in pattern is excellent versus any zone coverage because it high lows the curl zone. It is good versus man because of the flanker is running away from the corner

Quarterback: Takes a seven-step drop as he reads Stud and the strong corner. Versus a three-deep zone, reads Stud's reaction to the high-low. Versus man, throws to the best choice. Versus quarters, throws to the tight end or split end.

Flanker: Runs an in route. Accelerates on a vertical route to a depth of 15 yards. Plants on his outside foot and breaks parallel to line of scrimmage. Works to the first window and sits in the dead spot of the zone. Moves back toward the ball when the pass is thrown.

Tight End: Reads Stud as he runs a quick, diagonal five-yard out. If Stud blitzes, he should immediately look for the ball. If Stud runs to one and ignores the tight end, tight end will look for the ball when he arrives at his five-yard landmark.

Split End: Runs a dig route. Attacks the outside shoulder of the cornerback as he runs vertically for 10 yards. At 10 yards, receiver will break toward the post for five more yards. At 15 yards, the receiver will flatten and run perpendicular to the line of scrimmage.

Fullback: Blocks the strong tandem if he blitzes. If strong tandem drops into coverage, fullback will check Stud. If both defenders drop into coverage, fullback will run a five-yard hook route.

Tailback: Blocks Whip if he blitzes. If Whip drops into coverage, tailback will run a three-yard out route.

Coaching Points: The pattern adapts well to play-action schemes. Best results are attained when the pass is thrown to the wideside of the field. Tight end is the quarterback's hot read if Stud blitzes.

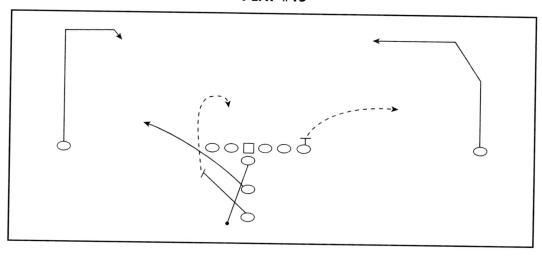

Purpose: This in pattern is excellent versus any zone coverage because it high-lows the curl zone. It is good versus man because the split ends is running away from the cornerback.

Quarterback: Takes a seven-step drop as he reads Whip and the weak corner. Versus a three-deep zone, reads Whip's reaction to the high low. Versus man, throws to the best choice. Versus quarters, throws to the fullback or flanker.

Flanker: Runs a dig route. Attacks the outside shoulder of the cornerback as he runs vertically for 10 yards. At 10 yards, receiver will break toward the post for five more yards. At 15 yards, the receiver will flatten and run perpendicular to the line of scrimmage.

Tight End: Blocks Stud. If Stud drops into coverage, tight end runs a three-yard outlet route into the flats.

Split End: Runs an in route. Accelerates on a vertical route to a depth of 15 yards. Plants on his outside foot and breaks parallel to line of scrimmage. Works to the first window and sits in the dead spot of the zone. Moves back toward the ball when the pass is thrown.

Fullback: Reads Whip as he quickly releases into the flats. If Whip blitzes, he is the hot receiver and should immediately look for the ball. If Whip runs to one and ignores him, fullback will look for the ball when he arrives at his five-yard landmark.

Tailback: Blocks the weak tandem if he blitzes. If weak tandem drops into coverage, tailback will run a five-yard hook route.

Coaching Points: This concept can also be applied to the pattern illustrated in Diagram 11-11 The split end would simply run a comeback instead of a dig. The pattern adapts well to play-action schemes. Best results are attained when the pass is thrown to the wideside of the field.

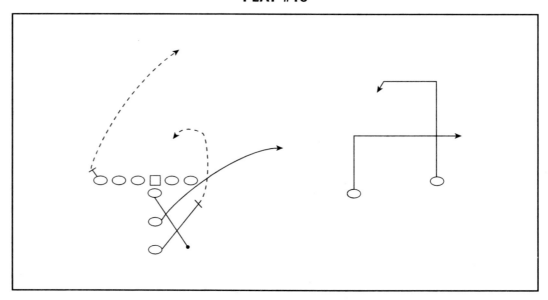

Purpose: This pattern provides the offense horizontal stretch of the flats and a high-low of the curl zone. It is particularly effective versus a three-deep zone.

Quarterback: Takes a seven-step drop as he reads Whip and the weakside corner. Versus a three-deep zone has the option of throwing the split end/fullback high-low or throwing the out to the flanker. Should stick with the fullback versus quarters and man.

Flanker: Attacks Whip. Speed cuts on his fourth step. Snaps his head around and immediately looks for the ball. Continues to stretch the defense horizontally if the ball is not thrown to him after his break.

Tight End: Blocks Stud if he blitzes. If Stud drops into coverage, tight end runs directly at the free safety.

Split End: Runs an in route. Accelerates on a vertical route to a depth of 15 yards. Plants on his outside foot and breaks parallel to line of scrimmage. Works to the first window and sits in the dead spot of the zone. Moves back toward the ball when the pass is thrown.

Fullback: Releases into the flats. Works diagonally until he reaches a vertical depth of three to five yards.

Tailback: Blocks the weak tandem if he blitzes. If weak tandem drops into coverage, tailback will run a five-yard hook route.

Coaching Points: The pattern adapts well to play-action schemes.

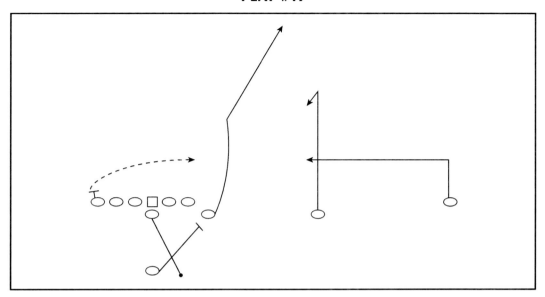

Purpose: This pattern provides the offense a high-low of the curl zone. It is effective versus both two-deep and three-deep zones. The fullback's flag route prevents anyone from playing over the top of the high-low.

Quarterback: Takes a seven-step drop as he reads Whip. If Whip plays the flanker's route, quarterback throws to the split end. If Whip squats, quarterback throws to the flanker.

Flanker: Lines up in the slot and runs a curl pattern. Attacks the outside shoulder of Whip and works vertically to a depth of 16 yards. Plants on his outside foot and shows the quarterback his numbers by snapping his head and inside elbow back toward the line of scrimmage. Works back toward the quarterback or shuffles laterally into a window.

Tight End: Blocks Stud if he blitzes. If Stud drops into coverage, tight end runs a shallow drag route.

Split End: Runs an in route. Accelerates on a vertical route four yards. Selling the vertical route is a must versus a backpedaling cornerback. At a depth of five yards, receiver plants on his outside foot and breaks parallel to line of scrimmage.

Fullback: Lines up in a tight slot position and runs a flag route. Releases outside and pushes vertically for 10 to 12 yards. Plants on his inside foot and simultaneously gives an inside head and shoulder nod. Accelerates as he angles out to an 18-yard-deep landmark.

Tailback: Blocks the first defender outside of the AST's block. Helps inside if this defender drops into coverage.

Coaching Points: Best results are achieved when the pattern is thrown from the hash toward the wideside of the field.

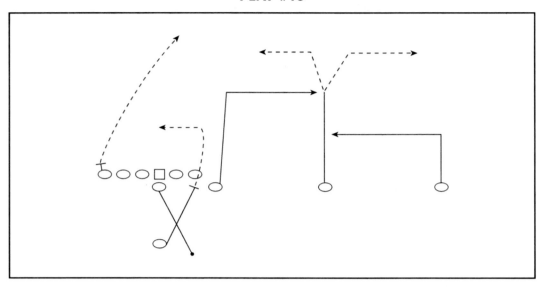

Purpose: This pattern provides the offense a high-low of the curl zone. It is effective versus both two-deep and three-deep zones. Flanker will read the coverage and break his pattern accordingly.

Quarterback: Takes a seven-step drop as he reads Whip. If Whip plays the fullback's route, quarterback throws to the split end. If Whip squats, quarterback throws to the fullback.

Flanker: Lines up in the slot and adjusts his pattern according to the coverage. Attacks the outside shoulder of Whip and works vertically to a depth of 10 yards. Versus cover 2, receiver will break to the flag for five yards and then flatten parallel to line. Versus cover 3, receiver will break to the post for five yards and then flatten parallel to line.

Tight End: Blocks Stud if he blitzes. If Stud drops into coverage, tight end runs directly at the free safety.

Split End: Runs an in route. Accelerates on a vertical route four yards. Selling the vertical route is a must versus a backpedaling cornerback. At a depth of five yards, receiver plants on his outside foot and breaks parallel to line of scrimmage.

Fullback: Lines up in a tight slot position and runs a deep out route. Releases outside and pushes vertically for 12 to 14 yards. Plants on his inside foot accelerates parallel to the line of scrimmage.

Tailback: Blocks the first defender outside of the AST's block. If this defender drops into coverage, tailback runs a five-yard hook.

Coaching Points: Best results are achieved when the pattern is thrown from the hash toward the wideside of the field.

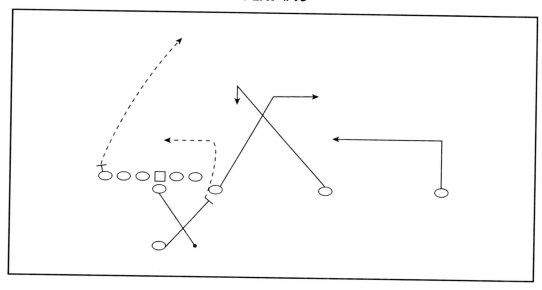

Purpose: This pattern provides the offense a high-low of the curl zone. It is effective versus both two-deep and three-deep zones. The flanker's route prevents the inside linebacker from dropping into the curl. The crossing routes of the flanker and fullback may burden man coverage.

Quarterback: Takes a seven-step drop as he reads Whip. If Whip plays the fullback's route, quarterback throws to the split end. If Whip squats, quarterback throws to the fullback.

Flanker: Lines up in the slot and immediately releases into the hook zone 10 to 12 yards deep. Meshes with the fullback.

Tight End: Blocks Stud if he blitzes. If Stud drops into coverage, tight end runs directly at the free safety.

Split End: Runs an in route. Accelerates on a vertical route four yards. Selling the vertical route is a must versus a backpedaling cornerback. At a depth of five yards, receiver plants on his outside foot and breaks parallel to line of scrimmage.

Fullback: Lines up in a tight slot position and runs a deep out route. Releases laterally and pushes vertically for 12 to 14 yards. Meshes with the flanker as he gains vertical depth. Plants on his inside foot accelerates parallel to the line of scrimmage.

Tailback: Blocks the first defender outside of the AST's block. If this defender drops into coverage, tailback runs a five-yard hook.

Coaching Points: Best results are achieved when the pattern is thrown from the hash toward the wideside of the field.

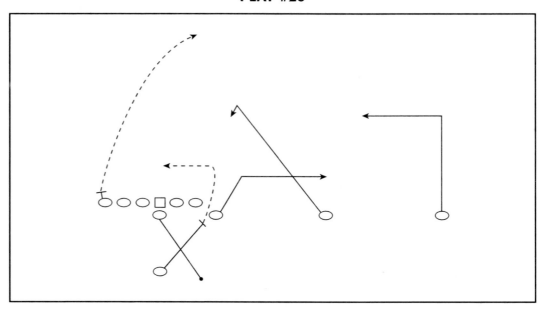

Purpose: This pattern is variation of the previous pattern; it also provides the offense with a high-low of the curl zone. It is effective versus any type of zone defense. The flanker's route prevents the inside linebacker from dropping into the curl.

Quarterback: Takes a seven-step drop as he reads Whip. If Whip plays the fullback's route, quarterback throws to the split end. If Whip squats, quarterback throws to the fullback.

Flanker: Lines up in the slot and immediately releases into the hook zone 10 to 12 yards deep.

Tight End: Blocks Stud if he blitzes. If Stud drops into coverage, tight end runs directly at the free safety.

Split End: Runs a deep in route. Accelerates on a vertical route 15 yards. Plants on his outside foot, breaks parallel to line of scrimmage, and finds a window.

Fullback: Lines up in a tight slot position and runs a quick, diagonal five-yard out. Fullback will look for the ball when he arrives at his five-yard landmark.

Tailback: Blocks the first defender outside of the AST's block. If this defender drops into coverage, tailback runs a five-yard hook.

Coaching Points: Best results are achieved when the pattern is thrown from the hash toward the wideside of the field.

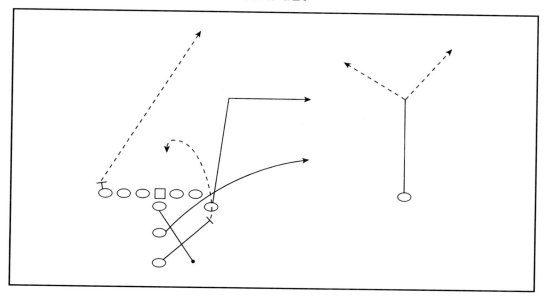

Purpose: This pattern provides the offense a high-low of the curl zone. It is particularly effective versus zone coverages. The split end will read the coverage and adjust his route accordingly; his primary purpose is to prevent a safety from jumping the flanker's route.

Quarterback: Takes a seven-step drop as he reads the defender dropping to the curl. When throwing to either the flanker of fullback, quarterback's aiming point should be between the base of the receiver's numbers and his hip.

Flanker: Lines up in a tight slot position and runs a deep out route. Releases outside and pushes vertically for 12 to 14 yards. Plants on his inside foot accelerates parallel to the line of scrimmage.

Tight End: Blocks Stud if he blitzes. If Stud drops into coverage, tight end runs directly at the free safety.

Split End: Accelerates to 10 yards as he reads the coverage. Breaks to the post versus cover 3 and runs a flag pattern versus cover 2.

Fullback: Releases into the flats. Works diagonally until he reaches a vertical depth of three to five yards.

Tailback: Blocks the weak tandem if he blitzes. If weak tandem drops into coverage, tailback will run a five-yard hook route.

Coaching Points: The pattern adapts well to play-action schemes. Best results are achieved when the pattern is thrown from the hash toward the wideside of the field.

PLAY #22

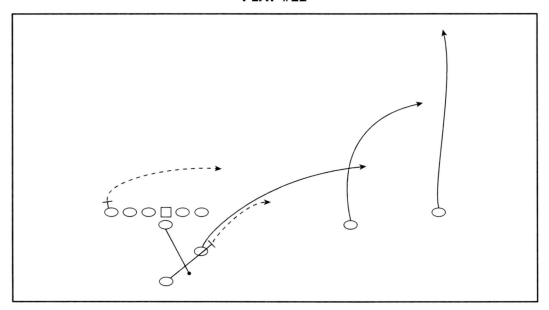

Purpose: This pattern provides the offense both a horizontal and vertical stretch of the flats by putting receivers at different levels in both the curl and out zones.

Quarterback: Takes a seven-step drop as he reads Whip. The quarterback must be schooled with the mindset that Whip must immediately retreat to the out zone or be beaten by the flanker's route. The fullback, in all likelihood, will be able to beat the weak tandem into the flats.

Flanker: Runs a deep banana route. Accelerates quickly and gets to an aiming point that intersects the split end's course at a depth of 18 yards.

Tight End: Blocks Stud if he blitzes. If Stud drops into coverage, tight end runs a shallow five-yard drag across the formation.

Split End: Quickly accelerates off the line and runs a go. It is imperative that the flanker drives the cornerback deep.

Fullback: Releases into the flats. Works diagonally until he reaches a vertical depth of three to five yards.

Tailback: Blocks the weak tandem if he blitzes. If weak tandem drops into coverage, tailback will run a three-yard out route.

Coaching Points: The pattern adapts well to play-action schemes. Best results are achieved when the pattern is thrown from the hash toward the wideside of the field. It might be better to align a slow fullback in a tight slot position.

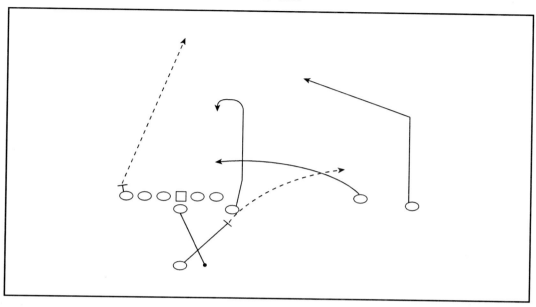

Purpose: This pattern provides the offense with a high-low of the flowside hook zone. It is effective versus cover 2 or cover 3. The flanker's route helps prevents the safety from jumping the fullback's pattern.

Quarterback: Takes a five-step drop as he reads the defender dropping to the hook zone (weak tandem or Mike). If this defender plays the fullback's route, quarterback throws to split end. If the defender plays the split end's route, quarterback throws to fullback.

Flanker: Lines up as the widest receiver. Accelerates vertically for 10 yards and then breaks to the post.

Tight End: Blocks Stud if he blitzes. If Stud drops into coverage, tight end runs directly at the free safety.

Split End: Lines up in the slot between the fullback and the flanker and quickly accelerates to a spot three yards in front of the fullback's original alignment.

Fullback: Lines up in a tight slot position. Takes the most advantageous release and then pushes vertically for 12 yards. Breaks inside and finds the window.

Tailback: Blocks the first defender outside of the AST's block. If this defender drops into coverage, tailback runs a five-yard out.

Coaching Points: This pattern can be thrown from any location on the field.

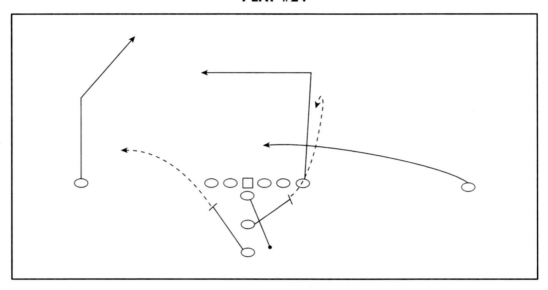

Purpose: This pattern high-lows the playside hook zone. The flanker's pattern, which is also the quarterback's hot read, is extremely effective versus man coverage.

Quarterback: Takes a seven-step drop as he reads the defender dropping to the playside hook zone. The flanker is the quarterback's hot read if both the strong tandem and Stud blitz.

Flanker: Runs a four-yard crossing route. Accelerates quickly inside. Versus man, he will run away from the cornerback. Versus zone, he will read the drop of the defenders dropping into the hook zones. If the defender dropping into the backside hook is waiting for him, the flanker will sit down in the playside hook zone.

Tight End: Runs a 14-yard crossing route. Takes an inside release. Pushes vertically for 14 yards. Versus zone, tight end speed cuts inside and finds the window. Versus man, he makes a good outside fake and gains separation by quickly accelerating inside.

Split End: Accelerates vertically for 10 yards and then breaks to the post. It is important that the split end prevents the safety from jumping the tight end's route.

Fullback: Double-reads strong tandem to Stud. Blocks the strong tandem if he blitzes. If both defenders blitz, fullback alerts quarterback by yelling, "Hot!" If both defenders drop into coverage, fullback runs a seven-yard outlet route into the playside hook zone.

Tailback: Blocks the Whip if he blitzes. Runs a three-yard outlet route into the flats if Whip drops into coverage.

Coaching Points: For best results, this pattern should be thrown from the middle of the field, and the flanker's split should be reduced slightly.

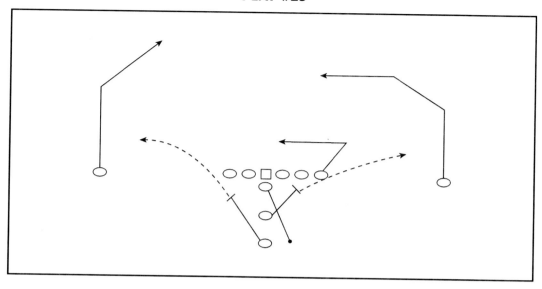

Purpose: This pattern high-lows the playside hook zone. Because the flanker's dig route is one of the most difficult routes for man coverage to stop, this pattern is effective versus both man and zone.

Quarterback: Takes a seven-step drop as he reads the defender dropping to the playside hook zone. The tight end is the quarterback's hot read if both the strong tandem and Stud blitz.

Flanker: Runs a dig route. Attacks the outside shoulder of the cornerback as runs vertically for 10 yards. At 10 yards, receiver will break toward the post for five more yards. At 15 yards, the receiver will flatten and run perpendicular to the line of scrimmage.

Tight End: Runs a delay route. Accelerates vertically and diagonally into the flats to a depth of five yards. Pivots back inside and finds a window. If he sees Stud blitz and hears the fullback call, "Hot," the tight end will continue into the flats and immediately look for the ball.

Split End: Accelerates vertically for 10 yards and then breaks to the post. It is important that the split end prevents the safety from jumping the flanker's route.

Fullback: Double-reads strong tandem to Stud. Blocks the strong tandem if he blitzes. If both defenders blitz, fullback alerts quarterback by yelling, "Hot!" If both defenders drop into coverage, fullback runs a five-yard outlet route into flats.

Tailback: Blocks the Whip if he blitzes. Runs a three-yard outlet route into the flats if Whip drops into coverage.

Coaching Points: For best results, this pattern should be thrown from the middle of the field.

PLAY #26

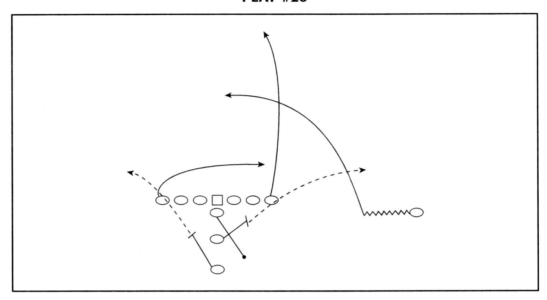

Purpose: This pattern high-lows the playside hook zone. The tight end's pattern prevents the free safety from jumping the flanker's route.

Quarterback: Takes a five-step drop as he reads the defender dropping to the playside hook zone. The split end (who is aligned in a tight position to the left) is the quarterback's hot read if both the strong tandem and Stud blitz.

Flanker: Goes into quick motion. As the ball is snapped, quickly accelerates to a position that intersects the tight end's course at a depth of 12 yards. Versus man, he will run away from the cornerback. Versus zone, he will read the drop of the defenders dropping into the hook zones. If the defender dropping into the backside hook is waiting for him, the flanker will sit down in the playside hook zone.

Tight End: Runs a seam pattern. Prevents the safety from jumping the flanker's route.

Split End: Line up in a tight position to the left. At the snap runs a four-yard drag across the formation. Looks for the ball as he crosses center.

Fullback: Double-reads strong tandem to Stud. Blocks the strong tandem if he blitzes. If both defenders blitz, fullback alerts quarterback by yelling, "Hot!" If both defenders drop into coverage, fullback runs a five-yard outlet route into flats.

Tailback: Blocks the Whip if he blitzes. Runs a three-yard outlet route into the flats if Whip drops into coverage.

Coaching Points: Pattern can be thrown from anywhere on the field.

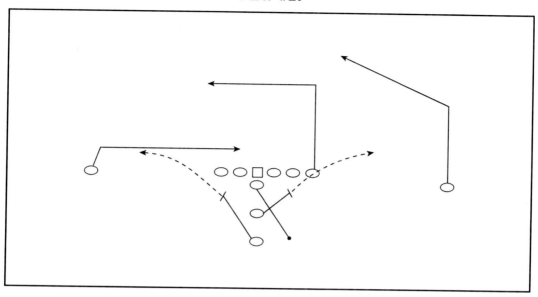

Purpose: This pattern high-lows the hook zone away from flow. The split end's pattern is extremely effective versus man coverage.

Quarterback: Takes a seven-step drop as he reads the defender dropping to the backside hook zone. The split end is the quarterback's hot read if both the strong tandem and Stud blitz.

Flanker: Accelerates vertically for 10 yards and then breaks to the post. Prevents the free safety from jumping the tight end's pattern.

Tight End: Runs a 14-yard crossing route. Takes an inside release. Pushes vertically for 14 yards. Versus zone, tight end speed cuts inside and finds the window. Versus man, he makes a good outside fake and gains separation by quickly accelerating inside.

Split End: Runs a four-yard crossing route. Accelerates quickly inside. Versus man, he will run away from the cornerback. Versus zone, he will read the drop of the defenders dropping into the hook zones. If the defender dropping into the flowside hook is waiting for him, the split end will sit down in the backside hook zone.

Fullback: Double-reads strong tandem to Stud. Blocks the strong tandem if he blitzes. If both defenders blitz, fullback alerts quarterback by yelling, "Hot!" If both defenders drop into coverage, fullback runs a five-yard outlet route into the flats.

Tailback: Blocks the Whip if he blitzes. Runs a three-yard outlet route into the flats if Whip drops into coverage.

Coaching Points: This pattern can be thrown from any location on the field.

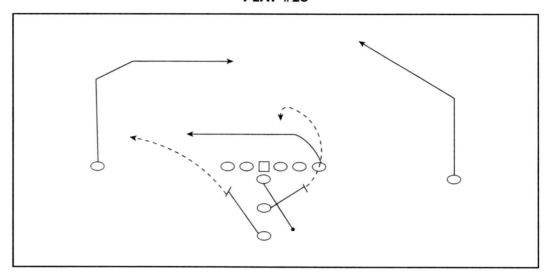

Purpose: This pattern high-lows the backside hook zone. Because the split end's dig route is one of the most difficult routes for man coverage to stop, this pattern is also effective versus man coverage.

Quarterback: Takes a seven-step drop as he reads the defender dropping to the backside hook zone. The tight end is the quarterback's hot read if both the strong tandem and Stud blitz.

Flanker: Accelerates off the line to a depth of 10 yards and then breaks for the post. If the safety jumps the split end's dig route, the flanker is usually open

Tight End: Runs a five-yard drag across the formation. Checks Stud during his release. If he sees Stud blitz and hears the fullback call, "Hot," the tight end will immediately look for the ball.

Split End: Runs a dig route. Attacks the outside shoulder of the cornerback as runs vertically for 10 yards. At 10 yards, receiver will break toward the post for five more yards. At 15 yards, the receiver will flatten and run perpendicular to the line of scrimmage.

Fullback: Double-reads strong tandem to Stud. Blocks the strong tandem if he blitzes. If both defenders blitz, fullback alerts quarterback by yelling, "Hot!" If both defenders drop into coverage, fullback runs a five-yard hook route.

Tailback: Blocks the Whip if he blitzes. Runs a three-yard outlet route into the flats if Whip drops into coverage.

Coaching Points: For best results, this pattern should be thrown from the middle of the field.

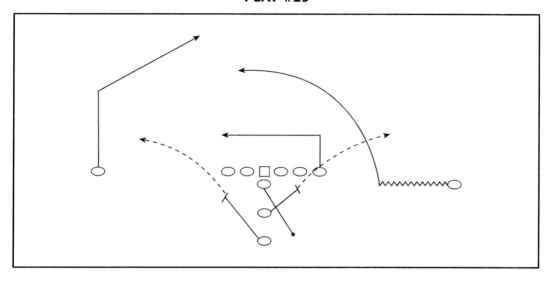

Purpose: This pattern high-lows the backside hook zone. The split end's pattern prevents the free safety from jumping the flanker's route.

Quarterback: Takes a five-step drop as he reads the defender dropping to the backside hook zone. If the free safety jumps the flanker's route, the split end should be open. The tight end is the quarterback's hot read if both the strong tandem and Stud blitz.

Flanker: Goes into quick motion. As the ball is snapped, quickly accelerates to a depth of 12 yards. Versus man, he will run away from the cornerback. Versus zone, he will read the drop of the defenders dropping into the hook zones. If the defender dropping into the backside hook is waiting for him, the flanker will sit down in the playside hook zone.

Tight End: Runs a five-yard drag pattern across the formation. Checks Stud during his release. If he sees Stud blitz and hears the fullback call, "Hot," the tight end will immediately look for the ball.

Split End: Accelerates off the line to a depth of 10 yards and then breaks his pattern to the post. If he sees the safety jump the flanker's pattern, he should make eye contact with the quarterback and expect the pass.

Fullback: Double-reads strong tandem to Stud. Blocks the strong tandem if he blitzes. If both defenders blitz, fullback alerts quarterback by yelling, "Hot!" If both defenders drop into coverage, fullback runs a five-yard outlet route into flats.

Tailback: Blocks the Whip if he blitzes. Runs a three-yard outlet route into the flats if Whip drops into coverage.

Coaching Points: Pattern can be thrown from anywhere on the field.

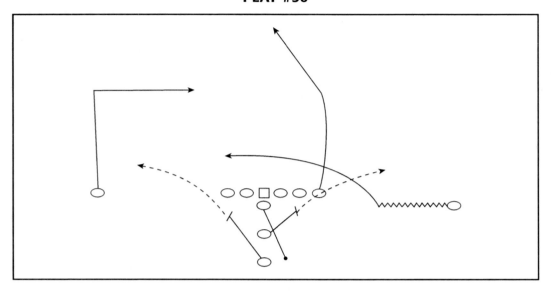

Purpose: This pattern high-lows the backside hook zone. The tight end's pattern prevents the free safety from jumping the split end's route.

Quarterback: Takes a five-step drop as he reads the defender dropping to the backside hook zone. The flanker is the quarterback's hot read if both the strong tandem and Stud blitz.

Flanker: Goes into quick motion and then runs a five-yard drag across the formation. Checks Stud and the strong tandem as the ball is snapped. If he sees both defenders blitz, he will immediately look for the ball.

Tight End: Runs a seam pattern. Prevents the safety from jumping the flanker's route.

Split End: Attacks the cornerback's outside shoulder as he accelerates to a depth of 12 yards and then breaks his pattern inside. Versus man, he will give a strong outside fake and then run away from the cornerback. Versus zone, he will read the drop of the defenders dropping into the hook zones. If the defender dropping into the flowside hook is waiting for him, the split end will sit down in the playside hook zone and find a window.

Fullback: Double-reads strong tandem to Stud. Blocks the strong tandem if he blitzes. If both defenders blitz, fullback alerts quarterback by yelling, "Hot!" If both defenders drop into coverage, fullback runs a five-yard outlet route into flats.

Tailback: Blocks the Whip if he blitzes. Runs a three-yard outlet route into the flats if Whip drops into coverage.

Coaching Points: Pattern can be thrown from anywhere on the field. It is important that the split end reduce his split slightly.

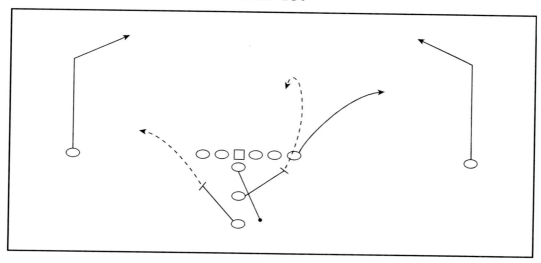

Purpose: The post pattern attacks the deep middle seams of a three-deep zone. This pattern should be taught in conjunction with the pattern illustrated in Diagram 11-33.

Quarterback: Takes a five-step drop as he reads free safety. When throwing the post, quarterback drills the ball to the receiver as the receiver is making his break. Quarterback should never loft the ball unless the receiver has gotten behind everyone. It is vital that the quarterback reads the coverage. Versus cover 2, the receivers will adjust to post-corner routes, and the quarterback will have to take two additional steps to insure proper timing.

Flanker: Runs a post route. Attacks the outside shoulder of the cornerback as he accelerates off the line to a depth of 12 to 14 yards (depth depends upon the receivers speed) and then breaks to the post. It is important that the receiver reads the coverage. Versus cover 2, the receiver will sight adjust to a post-corner route.

Tight End: Releases outside as he reads the coverage. Versus cover 3, the receiver will run a deep out (10 yards). Versus cover 2, he will run a seam along the near hash. Also checks Stud during his release. If he sees Stud blitz and hears the fullback call, "Hot," the tight end will shorten his out route to five yards and immediately look for the ball.

Split End: Runs a post route. Attacks the outside shoulder of the cornerback as he accelerates off the line to a depth of 12 to 14 yards (depth depends upon the receivers speed) and then breaks to the post. It is important that the receiver reads the coverage. Versus cover 2, the receiver will sight adjust to a post-corner route.

Fullback: Double-reads strong tandem to Stud. Blocks the strong tandem if he blitzes. If both defenders blitz, fullback alerts quarterback by yelling, "Hot!" If both defenders drop into coverage, fullback runs a five-yard hook route.

Tailback: Blocks the Whip if he blitzes. Runs a three-yard outlet route into the flats if Whip drops into coverage.

Coaching Points: The pattern can be thrown from anywhere on the field.

PLAY #32

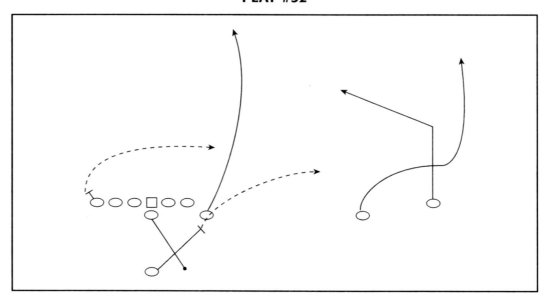

Purpose: This wheel pattern is a companion to the post pattern illustrated in Diagram 11-31. It puts intense pressure on deep outside zones of both cover 2 and cover 3 by creating horizontal stretch of this zone.

Quarterback: Takes a five-step drop as he reads the cornerback. The fullback's pattern should prevent the safety in both cover 2 and cover 3 from helping the cornerback deal with his dilemma.

Flanker: Runs the wheel. Releases diagonally outside to a depth of five yards and then races up the field and converts his pattern into a fade.

Tight End: Blocks Stud if he blitzes. If Stud drops into coverage, tight end runs a shallow five-yard drag across the formation.

Split End: Runs a post route. Attacks the outside shoulder of the cornerback as he accelerates off the line to a depth of 12 to 14 yards (depth depends upon the receivers speed) and then breaks to the post.

Fullback: Lines up in a tight slot and runs a seam. Versus cover 3, the fullback will attack the outside shoulder of the free safety. Versus cover 2, he will aim at a landmark one yard inside the hash.

Tailback: Blocks the first defender outside of the AST's block. If this defender drops into coverage, the tailback will run a five-yard outlet route into the flats.

Coaching Points: No sight adjustments are necessary for this pattern. Best results are achieved when the pattern is thrown from the hash toward the wideside of the field.

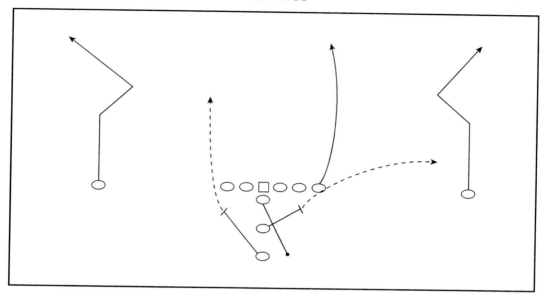

Purpose: This pattern is great versus man and cover 2. Versus cover 3, the quarterback and receivers will sight adjust to the post route illustrated in Diagram 11-31.

Quarterback: Takes a seven-step drop. Versus cover 2, reads the free safety. Versus man, reads the cornerback. When throwing the post-corner, quarterback will throw the ball to the outside of the receiver and away from the defender. The ball should be thrown slightly before the receiver makes his break to the corner. The quarterback must be careful not to put too much air under the ball and allow it to hang in the air.

Flanker: Accelerates upfield for 10 yards and then breaks to the post. At a depth of 14 yards, the receiver will plant on his inside foot and break to the corner.

Tight End: Releases outside and runs a seam along the near hash. Also checks Stud during his release. If he sees Stud blitz and hears the fullback call, "Hot," the tight end will immediately look for the ball.

Split End: Accelerates upfield for 10 yards and then breaks to the post. At a depth of 14 yards, the receiver will plant on his inside foot and break to the corner.

Fullback: Double-reads strong tandem to Stud. Blocks the strong tandem if he blitzes. If both defenders blitz, fullback alerts quarterback by yelling, "Hot!" If both defenders drop into coverage, fullback runs a five-yard outlet route into the flats.

Tailback: Blocks the Whip if he blitzes. Run a seam route if Whip drops into coverage.

Coaching Points: Best results are achieved when this pass is thrown to the wideside of the field.

PLAY #34

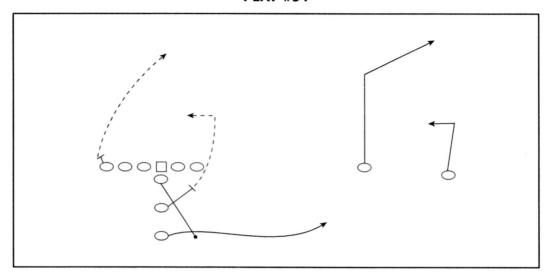

Purpose: This smash pattern provides the offense with a little different twist to high-lowing the outside sector of the coverage. The flanker's hitch route also servers as a counter reaction that exploits the backpedal technique of the cornerback, and the split end's quick corner route servers as a counter reaction that exploits the jam technique of the cornerback.

Quarterback: Takes a five-step drop as he reads the weakside corner. If the cornerback backpedals, the quarterback will drill the ball to the flanker. If the cornerback jams the flanker, the quarterback will throw the quick corner pattern to the split end. When throwing the quick corner, it is vital that the quarterback drills the ball and doesn't allow the cornerback to recover from his jam by hanging the ball in the air. The tailback swing route is the quarterback's last option.

Flanker: Lines up outside of the split end and runs a hitch. Attacks the outside shoulder of the cornerback. Takes three big steps, followed by two gather steps. Snaps his inside elbow and head around on fifth step and faces the quarterback. Keeps his head and shoulders upfield. Versus a jam technique, the flanker will work inside after turning toward the quarterback.

Tight End: Blocks Stud if he blitzes. If Stud drops into coverage, tight end runs directly at the free safety.

Split End: Lines up in the slot and runs a quick corner route. Attacks the outside shoulder of the Whip. Works vertically for seven steps and on his eighth step makes a hard inside move (especially important versus man coverage). He then breaks at a 45-degree angle toward the sidelines.

Fullback: Blocks the weak tandem if he blitzes. If weak tandem drops into coverage, tailback will run a five-yard hook route.

Tailback: Runs a swing pattern.

Coaching Points: This pattern can be run anywhere on the field.

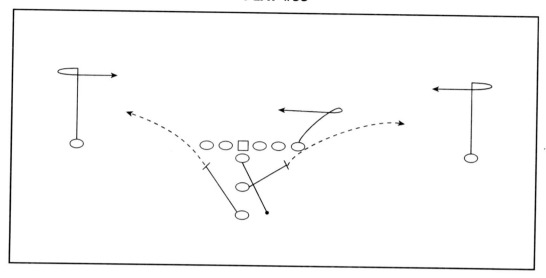

Purpose: This counter-punch pattern exploits the defender's reaction to the out patterns of the split end, flanker, and tight end.

Quarterback: Takes a seven-step drop as he reads the defender's reactions to his three primary receivers patterns. Drills the ball to his intended receiver just as the receiver plants and begins to reverse directions.

Flanker: Accelerates off the line and makes a speed cut toward the sidelines at 12 yards. Takes four more steps, plants on his upfield foot, and cuts sharply back to the inside. It is important that the receiver does not drift upfield after cutting back inside.

Tight End: Releases vertically and diagonally to the outside. After arriving at a depth of five yards, the tight end will take a couple of more steps, plant on his upfield foot, and cut sharply back to the inside. It is important that the receiver does not drift upfield after cutting back inside. The tight end is the quarterback's hot read. If he sees Stud blitz as he releases and hears the fullback make a "Hot" call, he will immediately look for the ball on his outside release.

Split End: Accelerates off the line and makes a speed cut toward the sidelines at 12 yards. Takes four more steps, plants on his upfield foot, and cuts sharply back to the inside. It is important that the receiver does not drift upfield after cutting back inside.

Fullback: Double-reads strong tandem to Stud. Blocks the strong tandem if he blitzes. If both defenders blitz, fullback alerts quarterback by yelling, "Hot!" If both defenders drop into coverage, fullback runs a five-yard outlet route into flats.

Tailback: Blocks the Whip if he blitzes. Runs a three-yard outlet route into the flats if Whip drops into coverage.

Coaching Points: Pattern can be thrown from anywhere on the field.

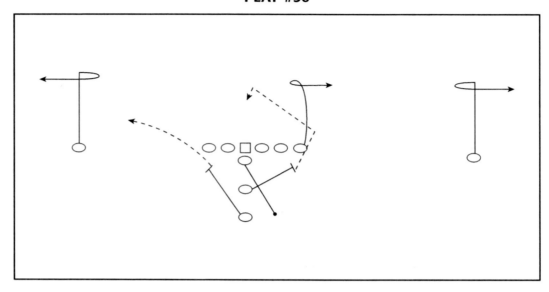

Purpose: This counter-punch pattern exploits the defender's reaction to the in patterns of the split end, flanker, and tight end

Quarterback: Takes a seven-step drop as he reads the defender's reactions to his three primary receivers patterns. Drills the ball to his intended receiver just as the receiver plants and begins to reverse directions.

Flanker: Accelerates off the line and makes a cut inside at a depth of 12 yards. Takes three more steps, plants on his upfield foot, and cuts sharply back to the outside. It is important that the receiver does not drift upfield after cutting back outside.

Tight End: Releases vertically to a depth of 10 yards. Makes a cut inside, takes three more steps, plants on his upfield foot, and cuts sharply back to the outside. It is important that the receiver does not drift upfield after cutting back inside. The tight end is the quarterback's hot read. If he sees Stud blitz as he releases and hears the fullback make a "Hot" call, he will immediately break his pattern to the outside and look for the ball.

Split End: Accelerates off the line and makes a cut inside at a depth of 12 yards. Takes three more steps, plants on his upfield foot, and cuts sharply back to the outside. It is important that the receiver does not drift upfield after cutting back outside.

Fullback: Double-reads strong tandem to Stud. Blocks the strong tandem if he blitzes. If both defenders blitz, fullback alerts quarterback by yelling, "Hot!" If both defenders drop into coverage, fullback runs a five-yard outlet route into flats.

Tailback: Blocks the Whip if he blitzes. Runs a three-yard outlet route into the flats if Whip drops into coverage.

Coaching Points: Pattern can be thrown from anywhere on the field.

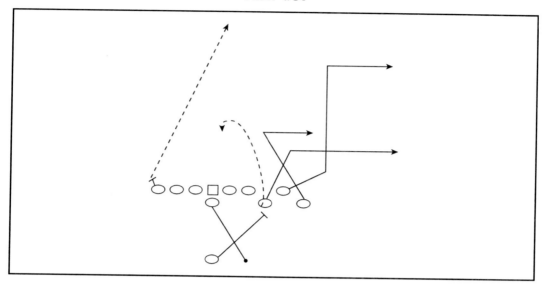

Purpose: This play is a mesh pattern in which the fullback and flanker run crossing routes so close to one another that they almost rub against one another. This pattern makes man coverage extremely difficult, if not impossible. The pattern also creates a high-low of the out zone.

Quarterback: Takes a five-step drop. Versus man, he reads the mesh. Versus zone, he reads the reaction of the defender covering the flats.

Flanker: Lines up in the wing position and meshes with the fullback at a depth of three yards. Continues downfield four more yards, plants on his inside foot, and sharply breaks to the outside.

Tight End: Releases to the outside. In all probability the defense will try to jam him. He must avoid the jam and accelerate to a depth of 12 to 14 yards (depending on his speed). He will then plant on his inside foot and sharply break his pattern toward the sidelines.

Split End: Lines up in a tight end position toward the left. Blocks Stud if he blitzes. If Stud drops into coverage, split end runs directly at the free safety.

Fullback: Lines up in a tight slot position and meshes with the fullback at a depth of three yards. Continues downfield two more yards and speed cuts to the outside.

Tailback: Blocks the first defender outside of the AST's block. If this defender drops into coverage, the tailback will run a five-yard hook pattern.

Coaching Points: This pattern can be thrown from anywhere on the field. The fullback is the quarterback's hot read on an overload pass rush toward the strength of the formation.

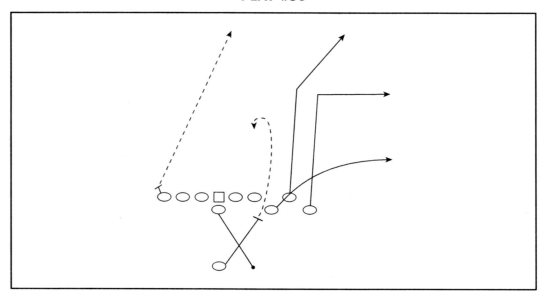

Purpose: This pattern creates a high-low of the out zone.

Quarterback: Takes a five-step drop and reads the reaction of the defender covering the flats.

Flanker: Lines up in the wing position and runs an out. Accelerates quickly downfield to a depth of 12 yards, plants on his inside foot, and breaks sharply to the outside. Versus man coverage, it is important for the flanker to make a strong inside fake before breaking to the outside.

Tight End: Releases to the outside. Accelerate downfield to a depth of 14 yards He will then break sharply to the flag. Versus man coverage, it is important that the tight end makes a strong inside fake before breaking to the flag.

Split End: Lines up in a tight end position toward the left. Blocks Stud if he blitzes. If Stud drops into coverage, split end runs directly at the free safety.

Fullback: Lines up in a tight slot position and runs a quick out. Accelerates vertically and diagonally to a depth of five yards and then continues toward the sidelines.

Tailback: Blocks the first defender outside of the AST's block. If this defender drops into coverage, the tailback will run a five-yard hook pattern.

Coaching Points: This pattern can be thrown from anywhere on the field. The fullback is the quarterback's hot read on an overload pass rush toward the strength of the formation.

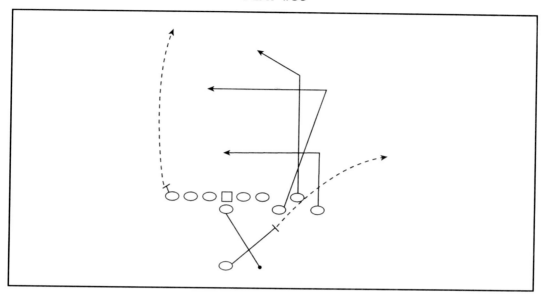

Purpose: This play is a mesh pattern in which the fullback run crossing routes so close to one another that they almost rub against one another. The pattern also creates a high-low of the hook zone.

Quarterback: Takes a five-step drop. Versus man, he reads the mesh. Versus zone, he reads the reaction of the defender covering the hook zone.

Flanker: Lines up in the wing position, releases vertically, cuts on his outside foot at a depth of five yards, and sharply breaks his pattern inside. He will then mesh with the fullback. Versus man coverage, it is important for the flanker to make a strong outside fake before breaking to the inside.

Tight End: Releases to the outside. Accelerate downfield to a depth of 14 yards. He will then break sharply to the post. Versus man coverage, it is important for the tight end to make a strong outside fake before breaking to the post.

Split End: Lines up in a tight end position toward the left. Blocks Stud if he blitzes. If Stud drops into coverage, split end runs directly at the weak cornerback.

Fullback: Lines up in a tight slot position, releases vertically and diagonally, and meshes with the flanker. At a depth of 12 yards the split end will plant on his outside foot and break sharply to the inside.

Tailback: Blocks the first defender outside of the AST's block. If this defender drops into coverage, the tailback will run a five-yard out pattern.

Coaching Points: This pattern can be thrown from anywhere on the field. The flanker is the quarterback's hot read on an overload pass rush toward the strength of the formation.

PLAY #40

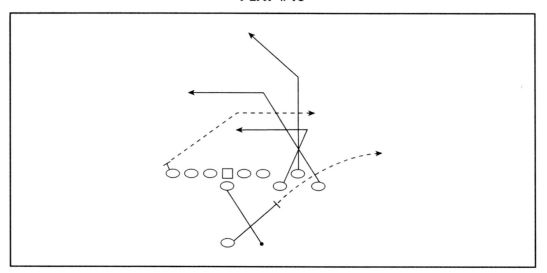

Purpose: This play is a mesh pattern in which the fullbacks run crossing routes so close to one another that they almost rub against one another. The pattern also creates a high-low of the hook zone.

Quarterback: Takes a five-step drop. Versus man, he reads the mesh. Versus zone, he reads the reaction of the defender covering the hook zone.

Flanker: Lines up in the wing position and meshes with the fullback at a depth of three yards. Continues downfield nine more yards and then speed cuts inside.

Tight End: Releases to the outside. Accelerate downfield to a depth of 14 yards He will then break sharply to the post. Versus man coverage, it is important for the tight end to make a strong outside fake before breaking to the post.

Split End: Lines up in a tight end position toward the left. Blocks Stud if he blitzes. If Stud drops into coverage, split end runs a 12-yard mesh with the flanker.

Fullback: Lines up in a tight slot, releases vertically and diagonally to a position that enables him to mesh with the fullback at a depth of three yards. Continues downfield two more yards and speed cuts to the inside.

Tailback: Blocks the first defender outside of the AST's block. If this defender drops into coverage, the tailback will run a five-yard out pattern.

Coaching Points: This pattern can be thrown from anywhere on the field. The fullback is the quarterback's hot read on an overload pass rush toward the strength of the formation.

12

Attacking the 3-3-5 with Screens, Draws and Shovel Passes

Screens

Screens are not just supplemental plays; they are a vital part of any passing attack. They slow down the pass rush and prevent linebackers from flying back into their zones. They also take advantage of the athleticism of wide receivers and running backs by forcing defenders to tackle them in the open field. No matter which of the many different variations of screen passes a coach selects, some common principles should be adhered to:

- The quarterback should not telegraph the play by looking at his intended receiver until the last minute. If the screen is based upon a seven-step passing action, the quarterback should sell the play by looking downfield during his first five steps and then gather himself and look at his intended receiver during his last two steps.

- Offensive linemen and running backs must also be actors; they must convince the defense that the play is a pass (or a run, if the screen is based upon a play-action fake). If the screen is not a quick screen, they must also be patient and not release to their assigned areas too quickly.

- If the screen is based upon a passing action, offensive linemen and running backs must do a good job of protecting the quarterback before they release to their assigned areas. Screen plays frequently break down versus the blitz because offensive linemen and/or running backs do a poor job during the initial phase of pass protection; consequently, the quarterback gets sacked before he has a chance to throw the ball.

- Screens based upon passing actions have a tendency to loose their effectiveness when the quarterback is unable to throw the ball downfield in clutch situations. Coaches sometimes attempt to conceal an inept quarterback by frequently calling a screen in a must pass situation. The defense is seldom fooled by this tactic.

The first type of screen presented in this chapter is the crack screen. This type of screen involves a pass thrown to running back behind the line of scrimmage and a crack block by a wide receiver. The wide receiver blocks the linebacker who is either responsible for covering the pass receiver man-to-man, or one who is dropping into the zone where the screen will be thrown. An important coaching point to mention regarding this type of screen is that the crack block must be thrown above the defender's waist. Diagram 12-1 illustrates a crack screen thrown to the fullback. When this play is employed, the split end will line up in the slot, work to the second level, and block the linebacker assigned to cover the fullback, or the one assigned to drop into the hook zone. Depending upon the defensive scheme, this player will either be the weak tandem or Mike. The quarterback will take a seven-step drop, and the fullback and pulling linemen will hold their blocks for three counts before releasing to their designated areas. This play is a good play to the wideside of the field.

A second crack screen is illustrated in Diagram 12-2. In this play, the quarterback is taking a seven-step drop and throwing the ball to the tailback. The tight end is flexed

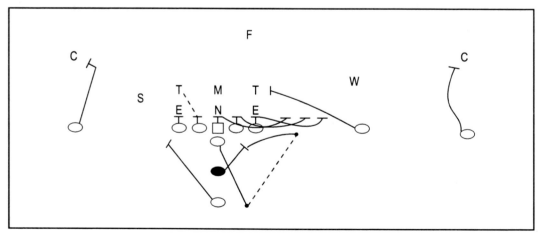

Diagram 12-1

seven yards and (depending upon the defensive scheme) he is cracking either the strong tandem, Stud, or Mike.

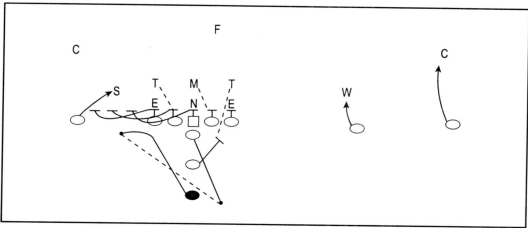

Diagram 12-2

A second type of screen that has become very popular in recent years is the bubble screen (Diagram 12-3). This play is thrown when the defender covering the flanker (Whip) is in an up position and the defender covering the split end is back. Its obvious advantage is that it puts the flanker in a one-on-one situation with the cornerback, who must make the open field tackle by himself. When this play is used, the quarterback will take a one-step drop and immediately throw the ball to the flanker. The flanker will bubble back and catch the ball behind the line of scrimmage. It is important that the quarterback throws the pass forward. If he doesn't, the pass becomes a lateral and if it is incomplete, the defense can recover it. The fullback is put in an up position so that he can easily block the weak tandem and not be in the quarterback's throwing lane.

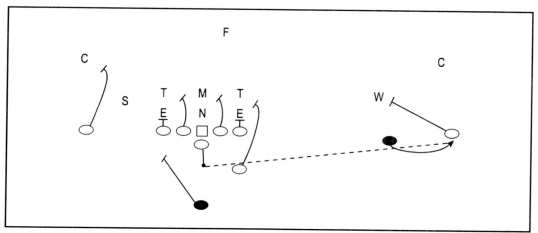

Diagram 12-3

Another effective screen against the 3-3-5 is the jailbreak screen. The play illustrated in Diagram 12-4 is a deviation of the norm. Rather than having three or four linemen release downfield, we have chosen to leave the flanker in a one-on-one situation with the free safety. Some might argue that this play is a variation of the bubble screen more than a deviation of the jailbreak, and they may be right. But, the illustrated play does give the offense excellent blocking angles which should insure success.

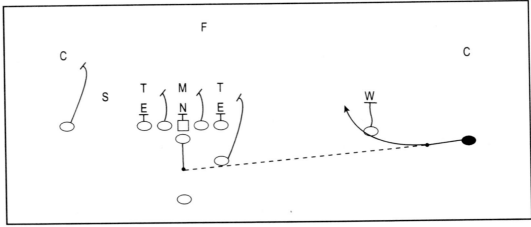

Diagram 12-4

The Shovel Pass

The shovel pass is a quick-hitting play that really takes advantage of a zone defense in which the linebackers immediately drop to their zones at the first sign of pass. One of the big advantages of the play is that the quarterback can simply throw the ball into the dirt and waste the down if something goes wrong. When executing the shovel pass (Diagram 12-5), the quarterback will immediately show pass, take three steps, plant on his third step, and softly toss the ball to the fullback with his left hand. The tight end will release and block the linebacker dropping to the playside hook zone. The ASG will check Mike, block him if he blitzes, and double-team with the center if Mike drops into coverage. The tailback will lead through the hole and block the weak tandem if he blitzes; otherwise, the tailback will continue downfield and block the free safety.

The Draw

Trying to figure out how to block the draw versus the 3-3-5 is both difficult and needless. The best solution to this problem is as follows: don't let your opponent run the 3-3-5 versus the draw. The easiest way to accomplish this preventive option is to line up in a trips formation and force the 3-3-5 into a seven-man front. Running the draw then becomes very easy. Diagram 12-6 illustrates the draw versus a forced 3-3-5

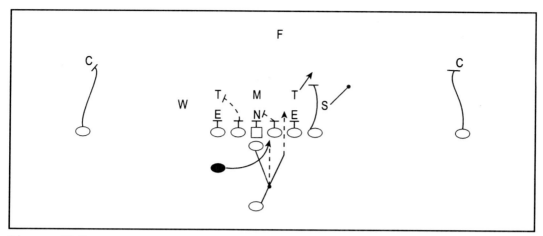

Diagram 12-5

adjustment. When running this play, the tailback will take two steps. His first step is a crossover step with his left foot that gains ground toward the line of scrimmage, followed by another step with his right foot. He will plant on his second step, pause momentarily, receive the ball, and then cut off the center's block. Some coaches may prefer to have the tailback take three steps.

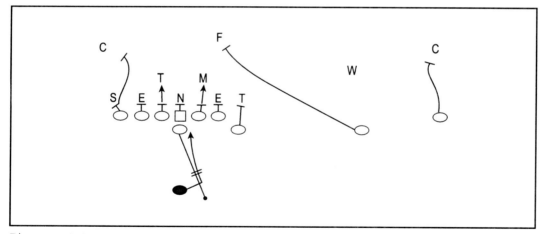

Diagram 12-6

Two screens that enhance the effectiveness of the draw are the fullback screen (Diagram 12-7A) and the tight end screen (Diagram 12-7B). Of course, a play-action pass could also be constructed utilizing draw action.

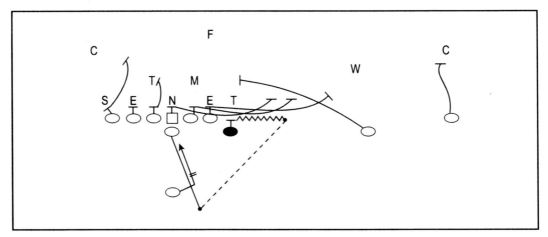

Diagram 12-7a

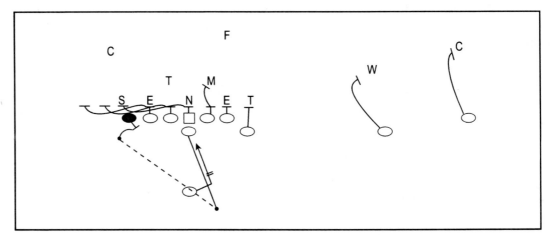

Diagram 12-7b

About the Author

Leo Hand assumed the position of the defensive backfield coach at Andress High School in 2004. In Hand's first season as secondary coach at Andress, the team had an 11-1 record and won a bi-district championship. They allowed opponents an average of only 7.7 points per game, had 20 interceptions, and allowed only three touchdown passes to be scored against them during the entire 2004 season.

Hand previously served as the defensive coordinator at El Paso (Texas) High School from 2001 to 2003. Prior to that, he held the same position with Irvin High School in El Paso, Texas. With over 36 years of experience as a teacher and coach, Hand has served in a variety of coaching positions in his career—achieving a notable level of success at each stop.

A graduate of Emporia State University in Emporia, Kansas, Hand began his football-coaching career in 1968 as the junior varsity coach for McQuaid Jesuit High School in Rochester, New York. After two seasons, Hand accepted the job as the offensive line coach at Aquinas Institute (1970 -1971), and then served as the head coach at Saint John Fisher College for two years. Hand has also served on the gridiron staffs at APW (Parrish, NY) High School (head coach); Saint Anthony (Long Beach, CA) High School (head coach); Daniel Murphy (Los Angeles, CA) High School (head coach); Servite (Anaheim, CA) High School (head coach); Serra (Gardena, CA) High School (head coach); Long Beach (CA) City College (offensive line and linebackers); and Los Angeles (CA) Harbor College (offensive coordinator).

During the last six years that he spent coaching interscholastic teams in California, Hand's squads won 81 percent of their games in the highly competitive area of Southern California. At Serra High School, his teams compiled a 24-1 record, won a CIF championship, and were declared California state champions. Hand has helped rebuild several floundering gridiron teams into highly successful programs. Hand has been honored on numerous occasions with Coach of the Year recognition for his efforts.

A former Golden Gloves boxing champion, Hand is a prolific author. He has written several football instructional books and published numerous articles. With his wife, Mary, Hand has nine children and 11 grandchildren.